[QUARTERLIFE SOLUTIONS]

Testimonials

"Jason Steinle has a gift: he puts himself in the places where he can learn the most and then he pays attention. In *UPLOAD EXPERIENCE: Quarterlife Solutions* he shares the stories he has gathered in an engaging and insightful way, offering us wisdom that can change how we see our lives, ourselves, and the world, regardless of our age."

—**Oriah Mountain Dreamer**, author of *The Invitation* and *The Call*

"If you don't define success it will define you. Jason Steinle will help you start out in the real world with the right foot forward. I highly recommend his work!"

—**Ed Brodow**, author of *Beating the Success Trap*

"Jason Steinle asks the deep, meaningful questions of life. Whether you are 18 or 81, I recommend his work to anyone looking to experience greater love and grace in life."

—**Marianne Williamson**, author of *Everyday Grace* and *Return to Love*

"Imagine a clear path to a life of adventure and dreams made real. *UPLOAD EXPERIENCE: Quarterlife Solutions* lights that path with the questions and answers that every young adult needs to know. A great contibution!"

—**Gay and Kathlyn Hendricks**, authors of *Lasting Love*

"The most difficult question in the universe is "Why am I here?" Sadly the majority of people never find their answer and live out purposeless lives. And that's exactly what makes Jason Steinle's work, books, and programs so immensely important—especially to our youth. With rare insight Steinle tackles this ultimate question and the key questions that spring from it. Wisely, he doesn't just share *his* answers; he shows us how to find our own.

—**Ian Percy**, MA, author of *The 7 Secrets to a Life of Meaning*

"Jason Steinle has gathered solutions to some of life's biggest questions. I recommend his work for anyone looking to create inner peace in the midst of a busy life."

—**Joan Borysenko**, PhD, author of *Minding the Body, Mending the Mind*.

"If you want to rush 'out there' to do your life, then rush instead to regard the questions that Jason Steinle asks—and find your answers and your happiest life."

—**Tama J. Kieves**, author of *This Time I Dance! Trusting the Journey of Creating the Work You Love*

"Jason Steinle has distilled the wisdom and advice from today's great visionaries. If you're ready to break through to new heights of personal and professional achievement, read this book!"

—**John Demartini**, DC, author of *The Breakthrough Experience*

"The secret to balancing your check book is to balance your life. *UPLOAD EXPERIENCE: Quarterlife Solutions* shows you how to live with more prosperity, purpose, and passion!"

—**Maria Nemeth**, PhD, author of *The Energy of Money*

"Today's leader must be authentic. We won't tolerate anything less. Jason Steinle provides you with the steps to reconnect to your soul and authenticity."

—**Gary Michael**, author of *Across a Crowded Room: From First Impressions to Authentic Connections*

Testimonials

"We are rushing around more than any time in history. I recommend Jason Steinle's work to show you how to get the most from today and to keep you on the right track, your track!"

—**Diane Sieg**, author of *Stop Living Life Like an Emergency*

"Jason Steinle gently 'mines' the gems of healing and wellness wisdom from a wide range of cultural creatives. His book is a must read for anyone seeking insight and answers for healing and for life."

—**Donald Epstein**, DC, author of *Healing Myths, Healing Magic*

"In order to thrive and not just survive in the real world, you have to be honest with yourself. Jason Steinle's work helps you look truthfully at your life and make changes for the better. I absolutely recommend his work for all those ready to move beyond the confusion in their lives!"

—**Cynthia Ryk**, developer of *The Art of Naked Truth*

"Why hesitate to change your life? It doesn't have to be difficult. Just read this book."

—**Ashley Lee**, 22

"It's great to know that other people are feeling and wondering the same things I feel. Jason Steinle's book is a great read!"

—**Caleb Foster**, 20

"Very insightful information that dares to ask the questions most teens and twentysomethings are scared to ask."

—**Marco Madrid**, 23

"One chapter and I was hooked. Jason has a wonderful, extroverted personality that he relates through text. I will be telling everyone I know to read this book."

—**Anthony Hamilton**, 22

"A great eye-opener for anyone questioning what they want to do for a living!"

—**Toby Cochran**, 25

"A lot of books we read today tell us what we should do. Jason Steinle's book helps individuals figure it out on their own. Jason presents ideas in a way that hits home and keeps people reading!"

—**Satana Gilbert**, 20

"Full of gems of insight, practical advice, and perspectives that open your eyes to the inspiration of time passing by."

—**Megan Eggers**, 28

"Jason Steinle asks some of life's toughest questions. What's more he has the balls to answer them."

—**Jay John Uecker**, 29

"Jason Steinle is aware of the big questions that face young adults. Dare to see how he and others have answered these questions and the difference it has made in their lives."

—**Jason Regier**, 29

"All will benefit tremendously from insight into Jason Steinle's unique perspective on how to go about life. I know I did!"

—**Chris Ewert**, 28

"I struggle every day with questions about life, the exact questions that make up this book. I highly recommend Jason Steinle's book, *UPLOAD EXPERIENCE: Quarterlife Solutions* to all of those who are looking for answers to any of life's challenges."

—**Mike Sletten**, 28

"I wish a book like this were available to me back when I was in my 20s—it would have changed my life!"

—**Katie Watts**, 34

"Absolute truth! For people who do and don't know their path in life, this book will either be a boost of confidence for you or the fire you need to get started on your journey."

—**Trent Alan Babish**, 23

↑ UPLOAD

quarterlife solutions

EXPERIENCE

FOR TEENS AND TWENTYSOMETHINGS

"I wish I had access to Jason's work 30 years ago!
A perfect gift for today's high school and college graduate."

[Jack Canfield, coauthor, Chicken Soup for the Soul]

UPLOAD EXPERIENCE:
Quarterlife Solutions
for Teens and Twentysomethings

By Jason C. Steinle

Published by
Nasoj Publications, LLC
Post Office Box 2367
Evergreen, CO 80437 U.S.A.
orders@UploadExperience.com
www.Nasoj.com

Copyright 2005 by Nasoj Publications, LLC

Cover and Interior Design by
Michele Renée Ledoux
www.mledoux.com

Photography by
John Formento & Jason C. Steinle
Except in cases where photo was provided by
individual and used with permission.

Photo of Lance Smith by Christopher Queen

UPLOAD EXPERIENCE is a Trademark
of Nasoj Publications, LLC

NASOJ

PUBLICATIONS

ISBN, print ed. 1-933246-03-0
Library of Congress Control No: 2004117052

Cataloging-in-Publication Data

Steinle, Jason C., 1976-

Upload experience: quarterlife
solutions for teens and twentysomethings/
Jason Steinle.—1st Nasoj pbk.ed.
   p.cm.
   ISBN 1-933246-03-0
1. Young adults—Life skills guides. 2. Young
adults—attitudes. 3. Young adults—Conduct
of life. I. Title
305.24—dc22

Printed in the United States of America

Do's, don'ts and myths

Do's

When you upload experience you *do* shorten your learning curve in life.

When you upload experience you *do* listen to others regardless of age, sex, and race.

When you upload experience you *do* have greater success in life.

Don'ts

When you upload experience you *don't* have to reinvent the wheel.

When you upload experience you *don't* have to hit rock bottom before you make a change.

When you upload experience you *don't* have to be old to be wise.

Myths

#1. "You can't upload experience because experience is something you must live through."

T or F

You can transfer the skills, knowledge, and wisdom of others into your own life. This is the basis of the apprenticeship method of learning.

#2. "Uploading experience is no different than going to school or taking a class online."

T or F

Uploading experience is *not* the same as acquiring book smarts. Instead, it's learning the lessons that others have gained through the school of hard knocks.

[UPLOAD EXPERIENCE]

Helpful Terms

upload (uhp'lohd) v. to transfer specialized information to a central center

experience (ex-pe'rience) n. knowledge or skill derived through the act of participating in an event

upload experience 1. to transfer the life skills and wisdom of another person into your own life 2. to instantly add to your life the knowledge and skill of others 3. to connect to the life experience of another person and integrate it into your own life

*-Tina **uploaded business experience** and received the first promotion in the company.*

*-Because Matt chose to **upload quarterlife experience**, he enjoyed his twenties and thirties.*

uplex (uhp'lex) v. to upload a lifetime of experience

upload experience number (a.k.a. uplex number) the total number of years of experience contained within a book, CD, or other information product.

*-UPLOAD EXPERIENCE: Quarterlife Solutions has an **upload experience number** of over 3800 years!*

[INTRODUCTION]

[TO MOM AND DAD]

Thank you for your support!

Introduction

Let's face it. Quarterlifers—people in their teens, 20s and early 30s—are overwhelmed. I know, because I'm one of them. Once we leave the protection of home and school, we are suddenly faced with many questions: "What should I do for a living?" "Where can I find Mr. or Ms. Right?" "What is my purpose?" "Who am I?" "How can I make money?" and "What is the meaning of life?" We turn these questions over and over in our heads as we venture into the real world for the first time.

It's not only the questions that are difficult. It's also the sheer number of them. Think about it. You're looking for the perfect career, making new friends, choosing a place to live, searching for the right partner, contemplating a family, exploring your spirituality, questioning the meaning of it all, and wondering if you can even survive. Wow! The irony is that we all go through this, yet few of us talk about it openly.

Just a few years ago, at age 20, I remember tossing and turning in bed at night with thoughts running through my head. I wondered why I seemed to be the only one who didn't have it all figured out. I couldn't understand how friends could already be getting married, committing to mortgages, and having children. I wanted to know why I was here on earth, and if my life mattered.

It's the same frustration, confusion, and uncertainty that led a classmate of mine to commit suicide by throwing his body off the lip of the Grand Canyon. Depressed and frustrated, he chose to end his life rather than carry on. In fact, did you know that our generation has the highest rate of suicide attempts? Recent studies linking depression to suicide found that depression has doubled among 20-year-olds over the past 13 years. When asked why, the director of one study said, "Times are more stressful, students are faced with more pressure, more decisions, and more competition. There is more demand put on young adults today."

Unfortunately, not only do quarterlifers have the highest rate of suicide attempts, we also top the charts in divorce, drug use, and alcohol abuse. Not to mention that from the time we graduate from college until we reach our mid-30s we seek a new job every year and a half, often in fields completely unrelated to what we spent years and tens of thousands of dollars studying.

Fortunately, my life changed the day I discovered that there are tools and techniques for navigating the real world. At the age of 24, I graduated from chiropractic college, moved to a new town, and opened an office. For the next six months I worked to build my practice, meet new people, learn how to run a business, find social involvements, stay in shape, and get to know my new town. I continuously felt stressed and full of anxiety. If you've ever had to give a public speech, do you remember that uneasy feeling of butterflies you experienced? I had that feeling 24 hours a day, 7 days a week.

It was that pain, along with the suffering I saw in my friends, which led me to pick up the telephone and call successful chiropractors and businesspeople. I began asking them what they had done when they opened their doors, and to my surprise they told me. Taking their advice, I made changes in my office and immediately began to notice positive results. Patients started signing up for care and referring family members to the office. Soon I was calling other individuals I admired and asking them questions about finances, relationships, spirituality, and personal growth. I took their suggestions, integrated them into my life, and experienced even more significant changes.

What started out as my personal questioning process eventually grew into hosting both a talk radio program and a talk television show. Now, each week, I interview the world's leading experts on the topics of personal potential, business, politics, wellness, spirituality, relationships, finance, and careers. These in-depth conversations with the greatest thinkers of our time have completely transformed my life. I wrote *Quarterlife Solutions* because I want to share with you what others have generously shared with me.

Imagine for a moment how your life would change if you had access to what the most successful people in the world know today that they wish they had known when they were just starting out in the real world. You do! It's in your hands.

By following the advice in this book, today I'm a blessed man. I own a successful chiropractic office and have started two additional businesses, my relationships with friends and family continue to deepen, I'm in the best shape of my adult life, I've finished a book,

I'm growing spiritually, and I have the genuine feeling that my life matters—I'm here for a reason.

Do I have it all figured out? No way! But my life is 100 percent better because I don't have the frustration, confusion, and uncertainty that I once did.

What if you were able to shed your frustration, confusion, and uncertainty? How valuable would that be in your life?

What this book has to offer you is a unique perspective. Not only have I brought together solutions from the experts, I've also interviewed over 300 of our peers. Each chapter contains the real life experiences, insights, and questions that other quarterlifers have shared with me.

Let me tell you a little secret. Our generation knows far more than we give ourselves credit for knowing. When I asked people 16- to 35-years-old to address the hardest questions that we face and heard their answers, I was amazed! In many ways their insights have had the greatest impact on my life. Here's why. Most of the experts I interview are in their late 40s, 50s, 60s, and even 70s. While you can't put a price tag on their advice and wisdom, they grew up in a different era than ours and can't necessarily relate to the problems, concerns, and obstacles of our generation.

Think in your own life about how easy it is to forget a problem once you've found a solution. Do you remember how much you agonized over which computer to buy? Once you bought it, all of your concerns became a distant memory as you moved onto the next problem. Now imagine how little of a problem you would remember if it occurred over 20 years ago. When I hit upon this understanding, I knew I had to focus *Quarterlife Solutions* around our generation and that's exactly what I did.

Each chapter is one of the major questions that we face as quarterlifers. There are 30 questions in total. While the book is designed to be read from beginning to end, you may find it best to go directly to the question you are dealing with right now. Within each chapter are the gems of advice that have been shared with me, along with my personal experiences and interesting stories taken right out of the headlines. At the end of the chapter is an opportunity section containing a tip, tool, or technique you can begin applying today to bring solutions to the very question being addressed. None of the chapters tell you what you have to do. Instead they provide you with the tools and information you can use to make the change for yourself. As one reader told me, "A lot of books we read today tell us what we should do. Your book helps individuals figure it out on their own. You present ideas in a way that hits home and keeps people reading!" Regardless of whether you read from front to back or pick and choose among the chapters, I promise that you will find clear guidance.

May this book change your life for the better as much as the writing of it has changed mine. This truly is the book that I wish I'd had when I was entering the real world. I look forward to the day when we meet in person.

Jason Steinle

Evergreen, Colorado

[CHAPTER ONE]

What is the real world?

"It was the strangest request I've ever received, but I ended up giving him permission to stay at home," said Fred Carcu's boss. "He seemed to be really scared of something bad happening on that day."

Fred, a computer programmer, never left home on Friday the 13th. In fact, he never left his home again. After announcing that he was staying in to avoid bad luck, Fred was stung in his kitchen by a rare wasp nicknamed "the wolf." The poisonous sting killed him on the spot.

You and I may not be as superstitious as Fred, but we can all relate to his fear. We've all felt like staying in rather than venturing out and risking being stung in the real world. The irony is that, like Friday the 13th, we worry about the real world without even knowing what

exactly it is or why we should be concerned.

MTV changed the face of television when it launched *The Real World* reality show in 1992. The now-famous first season, filmed in New York, opened each week with: "This is the true story of seven strangers picked to live in a house and have their lives taped. Find out what happens when people stop being polite and start getting real." More than a decade later, MTV continues to bring together people from around the world under one roof. From the comfort of our living rooms, we watch love affairs develop, careers be made, fights break out, and stress take its toll.

Due in part to this program, the phrase the "real world" has become a part of mainstream culture. But what exactly is the real world? How

jessi babish, 22

hometown:
hayden, co

favorite food:
mashed potatoes

biggest concern:
will i be a great
mother? how do i
prepare for that?

best date advice:
laugh

favorite movie: of
mice and men

**what you wish
you knew two
years ago:** how
to be good at
communicating

life motto: treat
others as you
would like to be
treated

do we know when we've entered it? Does it happen at the age when you're legally able to drive? In my home state, that's 14 years of age. No kidding! I had classmates in eighth grade who were driving to school. Is it at 18 years of age, when you're able to vote and required to register for the armed services? How about when you turn 21? Is that when the real world begins?

From my experience, you enter the real world at the time in your life when you take the majority of responsibility for your life's direction. For some, this is as early as age 10. For others, it may not happen until they reach their 30s. Many would argue that they know people who've never entered the real world.

The difference between the real world and what exists before the real world is *shelter*. Parents and the academic world are the two most common shelters that exist. Parents can protect and guard their children for decades from having to face the big questions of life. I personally know people in their late 20s who haven't yet looked at questions such as "What should I do for a living?" and "Who am I?" because they've been so sheltered. Do you know anyone like this? Likewise, the academic world has a way of creating a mythical existence that only exists inside its walls. Bank loans and family savings are used to maintain a safe and structured life. As Abby Wilner, co-author of *Quarterlife Crisis* shared with me, "In school you knew how to succeed. You knew what to do to get an A and which classes you were going to take next year. Everything was laid out for you. Then all of a sudden you leave school and have to carve out your path from all these possible choices."

Wilner continued, "This is the quarterlife crisis. It involves assuming new roles and figuring out an identity in an entirely new setting. Basically, it is the transition from being a student into an adult. It involves: trying to figure out what to do with the rest of your life, who to spend your life with, where to live, how to afford living there, and all of the new responsibilities that never existed before in school."

What makes the quarterlife period so challenging is that we are entering the real world, a.k.a. the adult world, for the first time. We begin taking responsibility for our lives and often get overwhelmed when attempting to answer the big questions of life. Stephanie Gunning, my editor and co-author of *Total Renewal*, taught me a valuable lesson about this confusion. "Life is always uncertain," she told me. "You just get used to the uncertainty. When it occurs for the first time, it's hard. But once you realize you'll survive each new situation, you don't panic anymore. You develop confidence in your ability to learn to handle the unfamiliar."

I agree with Wilner and Gunning. The real world is full of uncertainty. No longer does your life have a clear grading system that tells you how you are performing. Instead, it is up to you to navigate your own way. This requires the confidence which you gain by taking responsibility for your life and realizing your life does not have to be the same as your best friend's or the guy's down the street.

3

matt hongen, 18

favorite food:
sushi and thai
cuisine

biggest concern:
that i pursue
some direction
in life that
ultimately
doesn't make me
happy

**worst date
advice:** go for
money

**what do you wish
you knew two
years ago:** that
two years ago
i had more free
time than i ever
will again

life motto:
karma, karma,
karma

Sara, a 28-year-old Peace Corps volunteer on the island of Grenada in the Caribbean, shared with me, "The real world is what you make of it. How you choose to think and act is up to you. I thought I was in the real world for five years post-college, while I was teaching, but I'm realizing now that the real world is really how you define it. For one person that might mean staying in your hometown, getting married young, and having babies. For someone else, it may be leaving everything he knows and traveling the world in search of enlightenment. For most of us, it's probably somewhere in between. I'm beginning to believe that the reality of the world is up to you and how you choose to open your mind and expand your world. You may choose to live in a world that's small and safe and comfortable. You may choose to live in a world that challenges you and makes you feel vulnerable, but provides you with plenty of learning opportunities. It's up to you. It's your world, so make it as real as you'd like it!"

It has always fascinated me how little we actually know about the world around us. According to research, of all the sensory information that's hitting our five senses at any given moment, 99.99 percent is disregarded as meaningless. That means that our reality is based on less than .01 percent of the world around us. That's not much when you consider that if you received .01 percent of $1,000 you would only get 10¢.

So what's real? It's the .01 percent to which we choose to pay attention. Many people notice greed, violence, and dishonesty. Others in the same situation witness generosity, acceptance, and love. It's just like having a television with 1,000 channels. Although you have a thousand choices you only get to watch one channel at a time. If you get stuck on ESPN you'll see the world as a sports game. Just as if you get stuck on the Cartoon Network you'll see the world as a cartoon. It is the same in life. What you pay attention to becomes your reality. It really is a choice. As the adage says—when you change the way you look at things, the things you look at change.

Opportunity

You enter the real world when you take responsibility for your own life, safety, and well-being. Part of this responsibility means choosing how you view the world. Most people allow others to interpret and choose how they see the world. Listening to talk radio in the morning, reading the newspaper at lunch, watching the evening news at dinner, and checking internet articles before bed are all ways we let others influence us. While ideally these would be unbiased sources of information, unfortunately they are not. Media is show business and depends on ratings to survive, which means the sassier, sexier, and more painful a story is the better it does. There is a saying in broadcasting, "If it bleeds it leads, and you have to be either the blood or the Band-Aid." The result of sensationalism is that you get a slanted and limited view of the world. In order to establish your own authentic view of the real world I recommend the following

rashida jolley, 24

hometown:
washington, dc

favorite food:
teriyaki salmon

biggest concern:
i am driven in
life to do all
i can to ensure
the physical,
psychological,
and emotional
health of our
youth.

life motto:
les brown put
it best, "take
a leap of faith
and grow wings on
your way down."

four steps to rid your mind of trash and take in new information.

The first step is to go on a news fast. For one week each month completely avoid any radio, television, newspaper, magazine, or internet news sources. At first you may feel like a breast feeding child who can't find his mother, but soon you will begin to notice a shift in your thinking. Instead of jumping into conversations with people about the latest news headline you will be talking and acting on your self-generated thoughts. This is essential for you to see the world through your own eyes.

The second step is to simply pay attention to what is happening around you. Notice how others treat one another, the quality of the air, the pace of traffic, the girl helping her mom across the street, and so on. Just pay attention! As firefighter and author Peter Leschak says, "All of us are watchers—of television, of time clocks, of traffic on the freeway—but few are observers. Everyone is looking, not many are seeing." When you are awake to what's happening around you then you will begin to form opinions and an understanding of the world based on your own observations and interpretations.

The third step is to travel. You will learn a lot more about your "world" by seeing and experiencing the "worlds" of others. By witnessing day-to-day activities in other parts of the globe you better understand your own behavior. From this varied vantage point you will be able to see and understand a bigger picture of the world.

The final step is to read the wisdom literature. These are the books that philosophers, saints, and leaders in the present and past have written. For a suggested list of wisdom literature books visit www.UploadExperience.com. By immersing yourself in the thoughts and concepts of our greatest minds you will expand your own view of the real world.

more from rashida...

what you wish you knew two years ago: that my father was going to pass away six months later. you see, my dad was so incredible that although i spent a significant amount of time with him, it still wasn't enough. if i would have known then he would pass away, i would have spent those last six months of his life soaking up his wisdom more.

lesson you learned as a miss america contestant: how important it is to be true to yourself. i also discovered talents i didn't know i had, such as the gift of communication. that experience launched my speaking career.

learn more about Rashida and her new CD by visiting ajolleytone. com

7

david roman, 23

hometown:
chicago, il

favorite food:
pork chops and
rice

favorite song:
everything

secret to life:
family

favorite movie:
scarface

life motto: don't
worry be happy!

edwin roman, 24

occupation: trying
to be a good
father and the
warehouse

favorite song: two
joints by sublime

biggest concern:
where to go from
here? what job?
should i get
married? how will
my nine-month-old
son grow up?

best date advice:
be yourself

secret to life:
when you find it
let me know!!

final thought:
life's too short.
try hard and be
true to yourself.

CHAPTER TWO

Does becoming a responsible adult mean life becomes boring and monotonous?

You've probably heard the slogan, "What happens in Vegas, stays in Vegas." Each year friends of mine visit the "City of Sin" because they know they can let loose without becoming fodder for town gossip. In Las Vegas, no one cares what you do or with whom you do it. My hometown of Sturgis, South Dakota, is much the same way. Every August the Sturgis Motorcycle Rally attracts over 500,000 Harley-Davidson riders from around the world. They grow out their beards, let down their hair, slip on black leather, get new tattoos, saddle up their Harleys, and take a ride to Sturgis—and that's just the women! At the campgrounds, crowds gather around signs saying, "Show your body!" or "Legally Blind: Don't leave me out. Let me feel your tits!"

It's not just the men who are getting in on the action; there are also plenty of women taunting men for a quick show. Beer flows into cups like rain in a gutter, as music blares from the band on stage. The Rally is also the only week of the year that many of the locals really let go. As a kid, I even remember seeing Boyd Blummer, my minister and the man who confirmed me, dressed in black leathers and a Harley-Davidson tee-shirt.

So, does becoming an adult mean that life is boring except for a yearly trip to Sturgis, Las Vegas, or Mardi Gras? Absolutely not. The key is to look at responsibility as an opportunity rather than a burden. Mark Albion, author of *Making Life, Making a Living,* gave me an insight that's had a profound impact

jamie mcclung, 18

hometown:
laguna beach, ca

biggest concern:
what i'm going to
do after i stop
modeling

best date advice:
don't order ribs
or soup on the
first date. you
will end up with
food on your
face and in your
teeth!

**what you wish you
knew two years
ago:** in the long
run, what happens
in high school is
not important!

read more of
what jamie had to
share in "should
i travel and
explore before
settling down?"

on my life. "Jason," he said, "as you get older you acquire different experiences and skills that can make life more fun. Growing up and becoming an adult doesn't mean that you have to lose being a kid. In fact, it's really an opportunity to do more of what you want. As an adult you can do it when you want, where you want, and even make money while you do it. No one is telling you when to go to bed, what to eat, or with whom you can play. Instead, you have the skills, resources, experience, knowledge, and opportunities as an adult that you simply don't have as a child."

It makes sense. We can do more as adults. **The key is to identify the same qualities of activities that we enjoyed as children and just pursue them in a bigger and better fashion.** Take 65-year-old Bill Bunyan of Kansas, for example. I bet he ate a lot of hamburgers as a kid because he set a goal of eating a burger in every one of Kansas' 105 counties. Why would anyone spend three years driving around on weekends just to eat a hamburger in every county? Beats me! It has as much appeal as a sexually transmitted disease, but for Bill it was a mission. Last year over 50 friends and strangers gathered as Bill accomplished his goal and bit into the final burger at Paddy's Restaurant in Sterling, Kansas.

Instead of looking at adulthood as a ball and chain, wouldn't it be better to look at it as an opportunity? Like Bill, you can decide to use your resources to eat hamburgers, to travel the world, to paint pictures, or to build a better mousetrap. Maybe people flock to Sturgis, Las Vegas, and Mardi Gras because they limit their playtime to 14 days a year instead of 365. Taking a two-week vacation is easy. The real trick is being able to let your life and work become your play.

Jessie James of West Coast Choppers has custom built many of the finest bikes that visit Sturgis each year. He's a guy who's found a way to thrive doing what he's loved since he was a kid. As a teenager James fought the law by stealing cars, taking them apart, and selling parts through his illegal "chop house" business. After getting

caught and ultimately spending time in jail, James escaped to college on a football scholarship, but the scholarship and his time at college ended following a knee injury. He then found himself traveling the world as a bodyguard and bouncer for the band members of Soundgarden and Danzig.

After a concert injury, James stopped touring and returned to his roots. This time instead of running an illegal chop shop he took his love of working with machines and founded his own custom motorcycle company in the corner of a friend's garage. Starting with no partners and no loans, he now has over 50 employees, a hit television show, and he crafts unbelievable bikes for the likes of Kid Rock and Shaquille O'Neal. What was his secret? A lot of hard work and finding a way to make a living doing what he loved to do as a kid, only this time legally and on a much, much bigger scale.

Brian, 26, has similar interests as James. Since he was 13 he always had a love for customizing cars, but he pursued a college degree in architectural design of buildings

carter h. dickson, 29

favorite food: anything with avocados

biggest concern: getting stuck in a routine that i can't get out of, and not getting to experience enough of the exotic and foreign

best date advice: learn to cook. a man who cooks will never be hungry or alone

what you wish you knew two years ago: you don't even know what stress is until you have kids (step kids) who drive.

despite his interest. "I was only a few months short of completing my bachelor's degree when it really hit me," Brian told me. "I had more energy and drive to come home to work on my car than to go to my internship and pretend.

"I thought, 'Why spend the rest of my life working all day and then rushing home and going into the garage to do what I really love?' It was a hard decision, but I decided to go into industrial design and work on cars. My biggest concern was time. I thought, 'I'm 25 and I should be at point X by now,' but I was just starting over. At first it really bothered me, but now I don't care. People put too many time constraints on themselves. They say I have to be out of school by this time, have a job by that time, and have children before this time. Says who? Society? Unfortunately, people really short change themselves. If I don't graduate until I'm 35 it's fine, because I am doing what I want."

Brian could have easily ignored his passion of fixing cars and, instead, been hired-on at the architectural firm where he was interning. It would have been the easiest option, but he wanted more. Sometimes to get what you want takes letting go of what you have. Brian let go of the career and salary four years of college had earned him to pursue his life-long interest of building cars. "Right now I feel good," Brian told me. "I get to do my true passion all day long."

Opportunity

Adulthood is an adventure when you utilize the abilities and the resources available to you. Entering the real world allows you the opportunity to experience the fun you had in childhood, only amplified. The key is to make your play- and work-time one and the same. There are four basics steps that you can take to make this a reality in your life.

The first step is to take out a pen and piece of paper and answer the question: *What have I enjoyed doing and believe I did well?* Take a moment and look back over your life including your childhood, teens, and your 20s. Taking activities from each time period identify a

total of eight activities and write them down.

For example:

1. Helped organize a school field trip in sixth grade

2. In charge of a crew at McDonald's

3. Led week long backpacking trips in the Rockies

The second step is to look at each of your eight activities and answer the question: *What was particularly satisfying about that activity?* As you look at the activities you highlighted try to pinpoint what was appealing.

For example:

1. In charge of a crew at McDonald's

   a. Responsibility of leading people

   b. Organizing and planning the schedule

   c. Satisfaction of meeting our time goals for service

The third step is to ask *What is the recurring theme in each of the activities?* At first glance it may not be obvious, but look deeper.

leila mlynar, 26

favorite food:
hot and sour soup

biggest concern:
my son's future

favorite movie:
big fish

best date advice:
don't hook up on
the internet

**what you wish you
knew two years
ago:** how easy it
is to get into
college

life motto: don't
stress on things.
even if it does
happen you wasted
all that time
worrying about
it.

See what similarities exist in the activities and what you found satisfying. For example, I found over and over that I enjoy leading and organizing projects that have a positive outcome.

The final step is to match a job, project, or career with the underlying theme you discovered above. When you do this you will find that life becomes less stressful and much more enjoyable. For example, I took my theme of leading, organizing, and having a positive impact and developed a radio and television program that revolves around real people offering real solutions for the real world. Notice that while what I am doing today has nothing to do with a field trip or McDonald's, it does have to do with the consistent themes of those activities that I found the most rewarding.

William Shakespeare wrote, "This above all; to thine own self be true." When you uncover and pursue that which is most satisfying, you will experience greater fun and fulfillment as an adult than you ever did as a child.

CHAPTER THREE

What is my purpose?

Jenny Fellner, a 24-year-old actress, has known since she was 4 years old that her purpose in life is entertaining audiences. I know because Jenny and I grew up together playing in the sandbox, riding our Big Wheels, jumping through the sprinkler, and even dressing up and acting out plays in my basement. From such simple beginnings, Jenny grew to pursue singing, violin, piano, and acting. "I fell in love with it instantly," she recalls. "I never got tired of having to practice piano. I was never one of those kids where you had to tell me to practice. I loved it! My idea of fun growing up was learning new instruments, singing *Annie*, and taking voice lessons." Jenny went on to play parts in high school and community productions before earning a degree in acting at the University of Northern Colorado.

Upon graduating, Jenny packed up her bags and waved goodbye to family, friends, and the wide open space of the Midwest, and moved to New York City to try her luck on Broadway. Like thousands of other young actors, appearing on Broadway was her life dream. But New York wasn't kind to Jenny. "At first it was complete culture shock being in the big city where the pace is so much faster," said Jenny. "I was working at the restaurant at night, coming home tired, and then auditioning during the day. It was so daunting."

Jenny received rejection after rejection. Month after month she worked as a waitress and took temp jobs to survive. Doubting her skills and talent, Jenny felt frustrated, upset, and even depressed at times. Nonetheless, she persevered. She continued to audition again and

mario avent, 25

hometown:
memphis, tn

favorite food:
cookies

biggest concern:
welfare of others

life motto: if
life hands you
lemonade make
orange juice...
meaning anything
is possible

best date advice:
never argue with
a woman because
you're never
going to win

secret to life:
never rush

again, always reminding herself that even for those 30 seconds of the audition she was getting a chance to do what she loved—singing, dancing, and performing for others. Jenny had no Plan B, no escape route. As she told me, "I have always known to the point exactly what I wanted to do. There was no other choice for me. There was no other option. Nothing else made me this happy. I just decided at whatever cost I had to be in New York, because this is where it happens. I would do whatever it took."

Suddenly, after a year of struggle, Jenny's life changed with one phone call. Her talent agent informed her that she'd been cast as the lead role in *Mamma Mia*, the current number one show on Broadway. "It was one of those really surreal, almost slow motion moments," said Jenny. "I remember looking around the room and taking mental pictures of the way everything looked. My agent and I cried together, and then the first thing I did was call my mom." Jenny had made it to the top! Since this breakthrough opportunity, she continues to enjoy and thrive on what she does because she is following her purpose.

The answer to the question "What is my purpose?" is perhaps the most important information you need as you head out into the real world. In my opinion, your purpose is the reason you're alive on earth. Each of us has something we are specially equipped to accomplish. Whether or not you agree, there's no denying that there are major benefits to figuring it out. Let me give you a sampling of the positive impact knowing your purpose can have on your life.

In 1960, Srully Blotnick began a study involving the careers of 1,500 business school graduates. For 20 years he tracked the careers of these graduates who were grouped into two categories. Category A consisted of people who said they wanted to make money first so that they could do what they really wanted to do later—after they had taken care of their financial concerns. On the other hand, those in Category B pursued their true interests first, sure that

money eventually would follow. A total of 83 percent or 1,245 graduates comprised the "money now," Category A; whereas only 17 percent or 255 fit into the "pursue true interests," Category B.

In 1980, after 20 years had passed, there were a total of 101 millionaires from the graduating class. Interestingly, only one came from Category A. The remaining 100 millionaires were from Category B: those who pursued their own interests first. Srully concluded the study by saying, "The overwhelming majority of people who have become wealthy have become so thanks to work they found profoundly absorbing. Their 'luck' arose from the accidental dedication they had to an area they enjoyed."

While one of the benefits of finding your purpose may be money, according to Marlys Hanson, a career consultant with over 25 years experience and author of *Passion and Purpose*, other benefits include heightened energy, improved health, inner fulfillment, greater job stability, rapid promotion through

sarah gray, 22

hometown:
tulsa, ok

favorite food:
sushi

biggest concern:
money

last read:
davinci code

worst date advice: talk about past relationships

secret to life:
enjoying it

final thought:
less is more

the ranks, and a willingness to put in that extra something that results in extraordinary accomplishments.

How do we find our purpose? In Missouri, the locals are having some problems with carp. These large fish are frightened so badly by approaching motorboats that they leap out of the water and have been flying into people's boats. Can you imagine seeing a 15-pound fish jump into your boat? Several of these fish have hit people, knocking one man out and injuring one woman—true story! Like the fish jumping into the boat, most of us want our purpose to find us. We want to be trolling through life and suddenly have our purpose hit us upside the head! We want to be like Moses at the Burning Bush, where God, in no uncertain terms, tells us what we are supposed to do. For some, like my friend Jenny, it seems to work out that way. For others, myself included, there's no moment of epiphany or eureka. **So what can we regular folks do to discover our purpose? Simple. We look for it.**

Ask questions. "What is my purpose?" "Why am I here?" Grab a friend, pad of paper, and a pen. Sit knee to knee and have your friend ask you the question "What do you want?" or "What is your purpose?" over and over again while looking you directly in the eyes and taking down your responses. After two minutes, you'll switch roles and repeat the exercise for the other person.

Mark Victor Hansen, co-author of *The One Minute Millionaire*, says this is one of the most powerful techniques he's found for helping people discover their purpose. "As you go through the exercise, pretty soon you get to your core essence," Hansen told me. "It only takes two minutes, and I've had doctors say, 'In all my education, 28 years, I never got that.' Right! Because no one ever asks them! What do our parents do? They say, 'My son the doctor or my daughter the lawyer.' They lay all that stuff on you, and you never figure out what it is you want."

I agree with Hansen. Beside the times you've ordered a pizza or decided if you wanted fries or a baked potato, have you ever stopped and asked yourself, "What do I want in life?"

Opportunity

It says in the Bible, "Ask and you shall receive; Seek, and ye shall find; Knock, and the door will be opened unto you." This is precisely how you are going to discover your purpose in life—by asking.

Read through the steps below; then sit down with a friend and go through this method for discovering your purpose.

1. Find a quiet, comfortable location where you will not be interrupted.

2. Sit knee-to-knee with a friend.

3. Place a tape recorder beside you and start recording.

4. For two minutes one of you will ask the other the questions: *What do you want?* and/or *What is your purpose?*

5. Once they reply, ask them the question again and again.

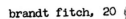

brandt fitch, 20

favorite food:
mexican

biggest concern:
doing good in
life

favorite movie:
new jersey drive

**what you wish you
knew two years
ago:** what i know
now

life motto: the
thing i live for
is what i'll die
for

6. Resist your temptation to start a conversation or make comments on what they are saying. Instead, just keep focused on asking the question while looking into their eyes.

7. After two minutes have passed, switch roles and go through the exercise again for two minutes.

8. When you are finished, grab a pen and paper and listen to the tape. Write down all the things you said you wanted. Look for the common ideas and similar interests in your answers and see if you can find an underlying theme. This theme is your purpose.

When you complete this exercise, some of you still will not be clear on what your purpose is. That's okay, the method is simple, but not easy. By asking the question you will have planted the seed for the desired outcome in your mind. Like entering the name of a missing document into your computer's search engine, your mind, heart, and soul will search to discover your purpose. It may not come to you immediately, but it will come.

CHAPTER FOUR

Is a life of purpose easy?

Lance Armstrong, the six-time Tour de France champion, was being interviewed on PBS's *Charlie Rose* television show. Rose asked him how he continued, year after year, to pound out top speed on the treacherous hill climbs for which the Tour is famous. Lance's answer was simple. "It is easier to live with two hours of pain on the bicycle than a lifetime of regret because I didn't give it my all."

There's a myth that once we find our purpose, life suddenly becomes easy and carefree, as if there'll be no more struggles. It's simply not true. **Finding your purpose gives you a clear sense of direction and a reason to go the distance, yet the journey may still be difficult.** Patrick Gentempo, founder of the Chiropractic Leadership Alliance, told me, "Jason, imagine that your purpose is to walk true north. You start out with excitement, but soon find yourself at a river crossing. It would be easier to change direction and go east or west, but you brave the rough rapids of the water in order to stay on purpose. Again, you continue to head north until you run into a steep and jagged mountain range. You know that the climb will be dangerous and difficult, but, to stay on purpose, you continue true north over the mountains. Next, you must cross a desert, followed by a swamp. With each obstacle you meet it would be easier to turn around, go east, go west, or even to stop. But the journey is not about whether it's easy or fun all of the time. It is about your purpose: heading true north."

I agree with Gentempo. For instance, last night ABC was showing the hit reality show, *The*

bianca hernandez, 18

favorite movie: the edge

biggest concern: if i'm going to get through college with flying colors?

best date advice: don't lead a person on if you're not interested

what you wish you knew two years ago: i wish i knew more about college and what courses to take

life motto: do what you need to do, then have fun

Bachelor. "I can watch just for 45 minutes," I thought to myself. "If you do, you won't get the chapter done or be ready for your interviews on Friday," my internal voice of reason countered. Back and forth I argued with myself, until the moment of truth. In the end, I kept the television off and wrote. Now, on other nights I get sucked into the Monday night game or the Thursday night line-up. There have been periods in my life where I actually locked the TV in my office basement so I would spend more time reading, working out, and writing, instead of watching television.

Certainly it would be a lot easier to turn on the TV than stay true to my purpose. Yet, nothing would ever get done. I know that my purpose is to assimilate information, simplify it, and share it. However, even though this is my purpose it can still be challenging to accomplish. This is where the irony lies. Oftentimes brief discomfort leads to long-term fulfillment. Likewise, short-term gratitude may lead to long-term regret.

Megan, 28, knows this is true. Two years ago she left a prestigious job managing five divisions of a company and became a waitress. Why? Because she wanted to have time to focus on what was most important to her—the relationship with her boyfriend (who's now her husband) and her family. Megan found much greater purpose in her close relationships than pounding out 60 hours a week at work. "I don't think a purposeful life is easy," Megan told me. "It's about doing what you feel like you're meant to do here. It's not always the easiest decision, nor the most comfortable decision to live your life with meaning, but it's absolutely worth it!

"When you live your life with a sense of purpose you feel more fulfilled," Megan continued. "I think cutting my salary in half and losing a tremendous amount of status were lessened by the sense of purpose I felt in doing them."

Like Megan and Armstrong, American cyclist Tyler Hamilton is another good example of staying on purpose. In the first stage of the 2003 Tour de France bike race, he crashed and broke his collarbone. The doctors told him the race was over, but he refused to listen. It certainly would have been easier and a lot less painful for Hamilton to watch the race on TV, but he knew he had more to give. So for 22 grueling days he rode with a broken collarbone. He even won the 123-mile final mountain stage of the race and came in fourth overall. Was this the path of least resistance? No. But I guarantee Hamilton is happier because he followed his passion to ride.

Sean Covey, former quarterback at Brigham Young University and author of *The Seven Habits of Highly Effective Teens*, shared with me a quote by Albert E. Gray. Gray spent several years studying successful people in hopes of finding out what they all had in common. His conclusion: "All successful people have the habit of doing the things failures don't like to do. They don't like doing them either necessarily. But their disliking is subordinated to the strength of their purpose." This is one of my favorite quotes.

tyler braithwaite, 28

biggest concern: that i have not or will not do my best or the best that i can

worst date advice: this could be the one. do what you can to impress her.

favorite song: anyone my children sing for me

what you wish you knew two years ago: life really is as hard as you make it seem to be

life motto: if you're not having fun, you're not doing it right

I have copied and pasted it on the wall in my home and office. The message is simple. A life of purpose is not always fun or easy in the short-term, but it is satisfying and meaningful in the long run.

Opportunity

A life of purpose transcends pain and pleasure. To live this life requires dedication and a shift of perspective. It certainly isn't the easiest route through life, but it is the most rewarding. I have found that one effective way of achieving this shift is to study the lives of those who were committed to a purpose. On the next page are several movies and books that I recommend. Just as you cannot stick your hand into a jar of honey without some of the honey sticking to you, by watching and studying the lives of purpose-driven people it will propel you to do the same in your life.

Is a life of purpose easy?

Movies

Gandhi

Gladiator

Rocky

Braveheart

8 Mile

Brother Sun, Sister Moon

The Fountain Head

Erin Brockovich

Patch Adams

Instinct

Guerillas in the Mist

Field of Dreams

books

Legacy of Luna by Julia Butterfly Hill

It's Not About the Bike by Lance Armstrong

Touch the Top of the World by Erik Weihenmayer

The difference between my generation and...
First of all I must explain that my parent are...
republican Christian fanatics. These views are...
confined to a narrow minded both...as...
and I can only view my opinion, me...
But my parents generation seems...
much more based on arbitrary m...
philosophy, and goal in life is...
get married, have children and...
education and a good capitalist...
in order to support their fam...
there is nothing wrong with...
Fact it is noble. But you co...
your life, and your ideas, an...
that that is what life is ab...
Just settle on that. We are...
being living in a complex world...
our own comprehension. My gene...
seems to be grasping that idea. W...
to be comming to the understo...
there is more to life tha...
represented to us. we are...
for more existencialism and...
more noble than raising a fa...
all you have in this world...
and we need to find that. Th...
is an endless search never s...
I hope that is true understan...
my generation. BCB

CHAPTER FIVE

What is the meaning of life?

What were you doing back in 1984? Like me, you probably don't remember and neither did Terry Wallis. In 1984, Terry was just 20 years old when his car swerved off the road and plunged into a river. The next morning he was discovered washed-up downstream in a lifeless coma. For 19 years following the accident, Terry remained in the coma—never able to lift a finger or mutter a word when family and friends came to visit him.

Can you imagine? What if one of your parents, siblings, or friends couldn't move or speak for 19 years? For some of Terry's family, like his daughter, who was born just two months before the accident, they had never heard Terry's voice. All of this changed, however, in June of 2003, when he suddenly regained consciousness. Like an infant forming his first words, the now 39 year old Terry spoke his first word, "Mom," followed by "Pepsi," and then a whole slew of words started coming out of his mouth. Soon he was talking and joking with family and hospital staff like nothing had ever happened. Everything looked promising for his recovery . . . except for one detail.

If you asked Terry who the President of the United States was, he would say, "Ronald Regan." Why? Because, Terry was stuck in the year 1984! To him Arnold Schwartzenegger had just muttered "I'll be back" for the first time in the original *Terminator*. Madonna was making it on the scene with her provocative hit *Like a Virgin*, and the Cabbage Patch dolls were all the rage!

Terry had lost the last 19 years of his life! As if he were Rip Van Winkle suddenly waking up from

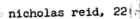

nicholas reid, 22

favorite song:
brushfire
fairytales by
jack johnson

biggest concern:
how am i going to
reach the goals
that i would like
to achieve in my
life?

best date advice:
just go with it.
don't try to make
it into anything.

**worst date
advice:** try to
adjust your style
to your date

secret to life:
enjoy it!

final thought:
don't let anyone
tell you what you
want to do is not
possible

a long slumber, Terry was just now re-awakening to his life. What if you lost the last 19 years of your life? What if you lost the last 5 or 10 years? What if you lost only one month? Unfortunately, this is exactly what is happening to many quarterlifers.

You lose your life when you fall asleep to it. When you become comfortably numb, it slips by without you ever knowing. The meaning of life, therefore, is to stay awake. When I asked Ed Brodow, a former actor and author of *Beating the Success Trap,* what life's about, he said, "It's about what you do from day to day. How are you spending your time? What do you do when you get up in the morning? You get up at 6 o'clock in the morning and go to bed at 11 at night. What are you doing in that time? Are you doing things that are meaningful to you?"

Throughout my life I have heard that the three "f's" are most important in life—family, faith, and friends. Margret McBride, co-author of the *One Minute Apology,* shared with me, "Life is about relationships. Nobody on their deathbed wishes they had gotten a better car, built an addition on their house, or had a higher salary. All of a sudden on your deathbed everything that is important comes to the forefront and it's about relationships with other people. A misspent life is when you don't realize how important the people that you're connected with are to you."

As quarterlifers we have a decision to make. On one hand we are told that meaning and satisfaction in life comes from acquiring riches, power, and fame and, on the other hand, people like McBride tell us that it is the relationships we have with family, friends, and God that are important. Both sides can seem pretty convincing.

Erin, a 25-year-old art teacher, and her husband have made their decision. Since getting married two years ago they have focused on family and time together. "I am not as financially motivated as a lot of my friends," Erin told me. "For a while my husband and I lived on only $8,000 a year. We certainly watched every penny, but we were not desolate by any means. Knowing I can live on very little income makes me confident that I'll always be fine. Sure, I like to be comfortable, but I'm not willing to give up my time with family to be super comfortable. I'd rather have to watch expenses and be happy."

While Erin and her husband have discovered their happiness in the simple life, her friends have taken a different path. "Most of my friends are very monetarily driven and they're happy," said Erin. "They have beautiful homes, fancy cars, summer cabins, designer clothes, eat at the finest restaurants, and take luxury vacations. That's how they find their happiness. It's wonderful if it works for them, but they work like crazy. I mean 12 hour days at the office all week long and then coming home and crashing only to go back in on Saturdays. I just don't relate to that at all. That's not my priority. My priority is to be with my family and to enjoy my life rather than just work."

Erin seems to have found happiness in the simple life, yet her

aisha mack, 25

hometown:
dallas, tx

favorite food:
pizza

biggest concern:
the condition
of the world and
if there will be
peace

favorite movie:
how high

**worst date
advice:** show up
with friends

**what you wish you
knew two years
ago:** to go to
school

life motto: keep
your head up!

friends will tell you the opposite. So as a quarterlifer, how do we determine the meaning of life when we've had so little life experience to draw from? The solution is not in whether you choose one lifestyle over the other, instead the solution is how you live the lifestyle you choose. Meaning in life comes from living consciously. It doesn't matter if you are running a company or raising a family, the real opportunity is how you live day to day.

It's not the big things but the small things that matter most in life. I really believe this is the secret. Too often we live our lives looking forward to the next holiday, the next promotion, the next weekend, the next home game and we end up missing a lot in between.

The greatest challenge you and I face in enjoying the details of life is that it goes against our biology. Let me explain. Our nervous systems have evolved to focus on quick, dramatic events and to ignore slow, gradual changes that occur over time. Just look at the events of 9/11. In a matter of hours the World Trade Towers crumbled killing thousands of Americans. This tragic event moved our nation. We cried together, rallied together, established relief networks together, and demanded something be done. On the other hand, did you know that according to the *Journal of the American Medical Association* each year over 106,000 Americans die from adverse drug reactions. A tragic event like 9/11 would have to occur every 2.5 weeks, killing 5,000 Americans each time, for an entire year to equal the number of Americans who die from adverse drug reactions, and yet as a nation we haven't rallied together to change this. Why? It's because the events don't capture our attention.

The adverse drug reaction deaths occur day-in and day-out in towns and cities across the United States. They occur in places like Orlando, Florida; Portland, Oregon; Sioux Falls, South Dakota; Durango, Colorado; Encinitas, California; and Burlington, Vermont. Because the deaths don't occur all in one location at one time, our nervous systems don't pay attention to them.

Just think about this principle in your own life. Chances are you're great at perceiving and responding to a house fire or deadline at work, but when it comes to watching the sunset or pausing to look into the eyes of a friend these are things you easily overlook.

It happens gradually, but eventually we no longer notice what is happening around us. We go on autopilot. In the morning we have the same conversation with everyone. "Good morning. How are you?" "Fine, thank you. How are you?" We take the same roads to work, read the same newspaper sections, watch the same shows, listen to the same stations, and think the same thoughts. We become zombies.

Terry was in a coma for 19 years. This occurs when the basic functions of the brain for breathing, heart rate, and body temperature still function but the higher areas which allow for thoughts and creativity are shut off. For 19 years he was "checked out" while life continued. How many people do you know who are doing the same

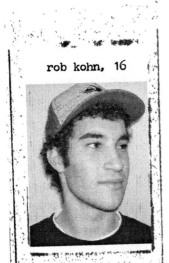

rob kohn, 16

favorite food: pizza topped with ranch dressing

biggest concern: that i will not work to my potential in high school, thus limiting my options for college and work post-graduation.

favorite movie: the boondock saints

best date advice: always be yourself and have a good time

worst date advice: maintain horrible hygiene and don't talk

thing? When you look around in morning traffic how many people are warm-blooded and breathing, but no one is home? How many of us are just going through the motions? Fortunately, you and I have a choice. We have the choice to continue to let life pass us by or at any moment we can step up and grab life by the horns.

Opportunity

The secret to a life of meaning is that it's not about awakening to your life; it's about staying awake. All of us have had the mountaintop experience where we are high on life. The real meaning of life is to take that mountaintop experience down into your job, raising a family, developing your friendships, and serving your community. It is the small things—noticing a friend's smile, making eye contact with a lover, watching the sunset—that give life its juice. In order to experience the small things and find meaning in life you need to live consciously.

I learned one of the best tools for living consciously during a conversation I had with a man when I was 20. He taught me to reflect back on the events of the day each night as you lie in bed. Starting from the moment you woke up that day, recall in as much detail as possible everything throughout the day. Remember the food you ate, conversations you had, streets you walked, music you listened to, and so on. The power of this simple exercise is that after a few days you will find that in the midst of brushing your teeth or talking on the cell phone, you will think, "Oh, I had better remember this for tonight."

Soon you will discover that you are observing more of your thoughts, choices, and actions as they are happening. You will become aware of the details of your life simply because you have trained your mind to pay attention to them. With this heightened awareness you are likely to taste your food and truly enjoy its aroma, to cherish a conversation with an old friend, and to relax in the warmth of a morning shower. This exercise will help you experience the meaning of life!

more from rob...

life motto: "don't think twice, it's all right" -bob dylan

what you wish you knew two years ago: the importance of music in one's life. being able to connect and relate to lyrics and songs should be something everyone can do. music in its entirety is now a very big part of my life.

favorite book: davinci code

secret to life: don't get too caught up in the moment, always be optimistic and perseverant because happiness and self-respect can guide you through even the toughest situations.

travis cox, 27

hometown:
newcastle, wy

last read: fast
food nation

favorite food:
pizza

secret to life:
find the joy
in all your
experiences

read more of what
travis had to
share in "when
should i have
children?"

mandy cox, 27

hometown:
springfield, sd

favorite food:
fresh salmon

biggest concern:
where is my career
going?

favorite movie:
sixteen candles

best date advice:
be yourself and
listen

secret to life:
everything in
moderation

[CHAPTER SIX]

Is life fair?

On Christmas Eve, I was visiting family in my hometown of Sturgis, South Dakota. As is our custom, we attended the candlelight service at the local church. Usually I find it comforting to return to my childhood church, but this year's service felt different.

The minister began praying for the men, women, and families of those fighting in the Iraq War. "Tonight we pray for the three American troops who were killed yesterday in Iraq. One of them was Chris Soelzer from Sturgis. May God be with him and his family." His announcement echoed around the sanctuary until it penetrated deep into my skull. Chris Soelzer, 26, was dead. He went to school with my brothers and me. He attended the same classes, walked the same halls, shopped at the same grocery store, and shared the same

friends, and now he was dead. Every day for weeks I had been hearing about my peers who were being killed overseas, but I had remained detached—until now. Suddenly it became very real. During the service it finally hit me that every man and woman killed is someone's classmate, friend, coworker, and family member. Dead at 26, is that fair?

On Veteran's Day, the *Washington Post* featured a story on Kenneth Dixon, 35, an army sergeant who has not stood on his own two feet since March 28, 2003 when his Hummer rolled as he was driving into Baghdad. Kenneth, now a paraplegic, is among many men and women in their 20s and 30s who are faced with forging a new life following debilitating war injuries. Not only is he in recovery, so is his family. Married and with

35

jane yoon, 19

favorite food:
italian

biggest concern:
family

best date advice:
be yourself and
don't lie

**secret to
life:** look at
everything in
a bright way
because tomorrow
is another day

favorite song:
bittersweet
symphony by the
verve

final thought:
live life to the
fullest, and live
in the moment
for it is gone
tomorrow.

two daughters, ages 12 and 14, to care for, Kenneth and his wife are planning for what will come next.

Why do some people live to be 90 and others die before their 30th birthdays? How come certain people get all the breaks and others have hardship after hardship? Is there justice and balance in this universe or is it a roll of the dice? Ultimately, the question we come to ponder is, "Is life fair?"

I asked Jason Dorsey, 25, who wrote and published his first book *Graduate to Your Perfect Job* before turning 19, if he thought life was fair. "Absolutely not! But you can control how you deal with it not being fair. Life always throws out unexpected twists and turns," Dorsey explained. "I don't think it's a matter of being fair or not. I think 'fair' is an arbitrary word. You choose how you deal with the challenges in life. Based on how you react you get new information and a new set of choices. That really is the key thing. If you step back and just watch it happening, it's all connected. The key is to realize you control how the dots fit together!"

Is life fair?

Erik Weihnmayer is a prime example of this. Born sighted, he gradually began to lose his vision, until he was completely blind when he entered his freshman year of high school. Can you imagine? Close your eyes right now and ask yourself, "What if I could never read the words out of a book again? What if I never saw another Arizona sunset, alpine glow on the Colorado Rockies, or green flash across the Pacific Ocean? What if I could never look into the eyes of my lover or watch another blockbuster movie? What if my world suddenly became dark?" This was Weihnmayer's reality. He went from sight to blindness because of a rare degenerative disease with which he was born.

Now Weihnmayer could have easily thrown in the towel and given up. He had every excuse but, instead he has moved ahead and achieved extraordinary things. On May 25, 2001, Weihnmayer became the first blind man in history to summit Mt. Everest. He accomplished this feat after already summiting the most challenging mountains in Europe,

North America, Africa, and South America.

I asked Weihnmayer how he has managed to progress ahead in spite of life handing him blindness. "There are questions we can ask ourselves that are dead-end questions," he told me. "The 'what if' questions are dead-end questions. 'What if' I could do things I can't do? In a sense, this idea of what's an advantage and what's a disadvantage is in your mind. I know that if I really analyzed the situation, I would probably find more disadvantages than advantages to being blind. So instead, I simply ask myself, 'How do I do what I want to do with what I have?' "

Weihnmayer continued, "That question has gotten me a long way. I just try to find advantages wherever I can. For example, I have heard people say I have an advantage when I am crossing over these huge crevasses on Everest because I can't see how far I have to fall. An advantage is whatever you think is an advantage in your mind. It is using what you have."

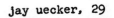

jay uecker, 29

hometown:
norfolk, ne

favorite food:
chicken fajita
burrito

biggest concern:
accomplishing
that which god
intended me to

**what you wish you
knew two years
ago:** it's going
to be fine. god
will supply your
needs if you
trust in him.

life motto:
if god is for
you, who can be
against you?

learn more about
jay by visiting
vitalistic
vision. com

Is life fair? Perhaps it is. Maybe, like Weihnmayer, we come into this world and face great adversity simply because it gives us the opportunity to overcome it. As a camp counselor working at Methodist and Lutheran camps, I heard visiting ministers teach, "God gives the greatest challenges to those from whom He expects the most." Surely this contains a truth because some of the greatest success stories have come from people who faced great adversity: Abraham Lincoln, Oprah Winfrey, Moses, Helen Keller, Beethoven, and Rosa Parks, just to name a few.

Likewise, if you believe in reincarnation, life is definitely fair. You are reborn time and time again to learn specific lessons toward your enlightenment. A hardship today is not a punishment but an opportunity to grow and move closer to self-actualization or nirvana. **The answer to the question "Is life fair?" really depends upon your mindset and beliefs. You choose to be a victim or a victor based on how you look at challenges.**

Opportunity

Life is not fair, but what you make of it is. You have the choice to learn and grow from each challenge that comes your way. I don't say this lightly but based on what Weihnmayer and others who have overcome tremendous adversity have shared with me. The following three steps are designed to help you see the order and opportunity in your life's hardships.

Step One

Reflect back on your life to the most challenging hardships you have been dealt. What were they? Write three of them on the top of separate sheets of paper.

Next, ask yourself what benefits you experienced because of each hardship. Do you think it's impossible to find any? Look closer. For example, losing your father at age six may have made you more attentive and loving with your own children because you understand that life can be short. Whatever your circumstances, look for the benefits that emerged. As you do

so, you will see that everything you thought was bad also had a benefit to it. Some benefits are easy to see and others take time, but they are there if you look.

If you embrace this awareness, it can create a major shift in your perspective. No longer are hardships roadblocks; rather you see them as intersections where you have new opportunities and directions to go.

Write down the benefits you've identified beneath the hardships.

Step Two

Write out the major challenges you are facing right now in your life. Use a new sheet of paper for each one. Realizing that no challenge comes without containing a benefit ask *What is a possible benefit of this situation?* Write the answers you find underneath each of your current life challenges.

Step Three

Again looking at your current challenges now ask the question: *How can I do what I want with what I have?* When you look closely

39

casey roberts, 22

home state: va

favorite song:
girls by the
beastie boys

biggest concern:
my brother and
friends going to
war

last read: the
madonna complex

best date advice:
don't do it.
don't date. just
have lots of male
friends.

favorite food:
pizza

secret to life:
my two year old
son. everything
is simple and
easy with him.

at what you already have, you will see that a number of resources are available to you. For example, you probably have friends with whom you can network, a strong work ethic, job skills that can be further developed, and a supportive family. These are just a few of the resources you may discover you possess.

Examining your resources shifts your perspective from lack and unfairness to gratitude. It is hard to be pissed off at life when you are constantly reminding yourself of all that you have.

Step Four

The final step is to ask yourself the question: *Is my life fair?* Ask this as you're looking back and seeing the many benefits and blessings that came from your previous hardships. As you do this be careful not to get caught up in comparing your life to others. As the famous poem "Desinerata" states, "Do not compare yourself with others for always there will be lesser and greater persons." Instead just be honest and discover for yourself if life is indeed fair.

CHAPTER SEVEN

Who am I?

"Yes, I have a lot of regrets. I lost my entire youth from age 16 to 21 running from the police and 21 to 26 sitting in prison. Being on the run was a very lonely life," said Frank Abagale, whose life inspired the movie *Catch Me If You Can*.

Abagale was lots of things to a lot of people. At age 16, he made a fake pilot's ID and started traveling the world. "I would basically board these planes and ride the jumpseat, deadheading from city to city, on different airlines." During these free trips, he cashed over $2.5 million worth of bad checks in the United States and abroad.

The airlines weren't his only con. Before he reached the age of 21, Frank had passed himself off as a surgeon in a hospital, a professor at a university, and he even tried and won a case as a lawyer, all while switching identities and conning people for money—and women for sex.

Eventually, the law caught up with him and Frank served hard time in several countries, including the United States. Ironically, because of his expertise, today he owns a company that helps financial institutions and government agencies protect themselves from forgery and embezzlement.

So, who is Frank Abagale? Some would tell you he is a pilot, a businessman, a doctor, a lawyer, a father, a consultant, a son, a lecturer, a writer, and a husband. It's true that he has played all these roles. But if you stripped these titles from him, who remains? Surely there is more to Abagale than a title or a role, just as there is much more to you than a degree, a position, or your relationship to other people.

mike sletten, 29

biggest concern: god (religion)

what you wish you knew two years ago: which stocks i should have bought, instead of the stocks that i did buy

what will you be doing in five years: working (hopefully not at the same job), raising my two sons, and enjoying my spare time with my children and friends

life motto: live your life one day at a time and be thankful for every day that you have

Robert Cooper, a former marine and author of *The Other 90%*, taught me to ask the powerful question, "Who am I when nobody else is watching?" When you take away titles like "doctor" and "professor," jobs like "auto mechanic" and "file clerk," sporting pursuits like "golfer" and "Bronco's fan," hobbies like "gardener" and "photographer," political affiliations like "Republican" and "Democrat," racial heritages like "African-American" and "Caucasian," family ties like "mother" and "uncle," and involvements such as "church member" or "volunteer" with what are you left? Who are you when you're just being you? It's a big question that can be hard to answer when you're caught up in the speed of life.

Angel, 26, found her answer when she departed on a two-month sailing trip across the Atlantic Ocean. "At sea, I had nothing to do, no place to go, no one to talk to, and I learned a lot about myself." For Angel, life had been flying for the preceding ten years. Living with a group of friends in New York

City, she worked hard and played even harder. But the late nights at the club and expensive furniture at home never fully satisfied her. It was while on the sailing trip that she realized a direction in her life.

"I saw myself as a speck in the middle of the ocean," says Angel. "I was overwhelmed by the power of the ocean. I felt small, but not insignificant. I was a part of a system that I could never overthrow, but I could work with. When you're sailing, you work with the wind, the water, and the current. It's like my Judo training, if you try to fight the ocean, you'll sink, but if you work with it, you can go anywhere."

This lesson made her realize that even with all the corruption and negativity in the world, she could still do her part to make the world a better place. Drawing upon her new sense of self, she began a career which utilizes her talents of communication, compassion, and bilingual skills to assist politicians whose views she supports campaign to reach new voters.

A college roommate once told me, "Jason, it's the clothes that make the man." At the time I had on oversized jeans and a baggy shirt. I remember thinking, *If clothes make the man, then I'm only half the man I'm supposed to be!*

The truth is that discovering who we are is an inside job. Advertisers spend millions of dollars annually to persuade us that a pair of pants, a beverage, or a brand of shoes will make us sexy, brave, smooth, or sophisticated. But these are all just wrappings on the true gift that resides inside each of us. When we discover this internal gift, we understand the answer to the question "Who am I?"

At the age of 9, Black Elk, an Oglala Sioux holy man, was on the verge of death. For 12 days, he fought for his life when suddenly a life altering vision was unveiled to him. It was a vision that he spent the rest of his life trying to understand and live, as he explains in the book *Black Elk Speaks*. "Nothing I have ever seen with my eyes was so clear and bright as what my vision showed me; and no words

amber hawke, 25

hometown:
lexington, ne

favorite food:
sushi

biggest concern:
what the world
will be like in a
few years when i
have children

**favorite
book:** power of
intention by
wayne dyer

life motto:
live life to the
fullest, take
advantage of
whatever life
offers, don't be
afraid

that I have ever heard with my ears were like the words I heard. As I grow older the meaning becomes clearer and clearer, and even now I know that more was shown to me than I can tell."

Over and over, I've observed that silence and nature are the two most powerful catalysts for discovering who you are. Black Elk found his answers through the silence brought upon him by sickness and the respect for the land that his people shared. Angel found hers through the magnificence of the ocean and the silence of sailing. It doesn't matter how the silence is brought about, it's only important that it occurs.

Jesus Christ spent 40 days and 40 nights in the desert. Mahatma Gandhi and Nelson Mandela deepened their convictions and identities while spending time in jail. Julia Butterfly Hill discovered herself while spending 738 days sitting in the branches of an ancient redwood tree in northern California protesting clear cutting. Air Force Colonel Norman A. McDaniel "had to search deep within" during

44

the six years he endured isolation and torture as a Vietnam prisoner of war. Eckhart Tolle was homeless and lived in a park for two years as he grew to understand himself and later wrote the bestseller *The Power of Now.* Even in my own life, I've seen the significance of silence and nature.

Much of my adolescence was spent archery hunting deer in the Black Hills of South Dakota. My friend San and I logged hours during the spring and summer scouting the behavior of the deer. By the time hunting season started, we had a good understanding of the deer and the woods. We knew where the big bucks lived, when they came out of the forest to eat and drink, and which trails they used.

Now, one of the keys to archery hunting is blending into your environment. To achieve this, San and I washed our clothes in baking soda, poured Doe-In-Heat Scent on our clothes, covered ourselves in camouflage, and rubbed our boots with deer droppings from the area. (Hmm, maybe that's why we were never really popular with the girls.)

Once the hunting season began, we'd sit quietly for hours at a time, sometimes in tree stands and other times on the ground. Occasionally, we would still-walk—walking very slowly and quietly—through the woods. In the afternoon, we'd each set out in separate directions from my truck, and we wouldn't see one another again until returning after sundown.

For me, the four hours I spent in the woods night after night were an unforeseen blessing in my life. When I sat down and shut up, I discovered that the woods came alive. I witnessed squirrels storing acorns for the winter, birds migrating south, woodpeckers building their homes, and deer carefully moving through the woods. The greatest gift of all though was the silence. Because any noise would serve to alarm and scare away a trophy buck, I remained silent: no radio, videogame, book, homework, journal, magazine, walkie-talkie, or computer. Instead, I had an alert stillness.

Though I spent hour after hour, day after day, year after year, I never

nathan dern, 19

favorite food:
soy milk

biggest concern:
smiling

**difference
between our
generation and
our parents:**
our parent's
generation
believed in
people more.
they recognized
that independent
movements,where
the power is
in the people,
is the way to
make change, not
relying on the
outcome of an
election.

bagged the trophy buck I sought. However, I did "bag" a tremendous amount of insight into my life. Sitting in quiet reflection, I heard the drumming of my own beat; a rhythm that gave me the courage to say no to some adventures and yes to others in my life. I've worked to hear this internal rhythm louder and clearer with each passing year. I'm absolutely certain that none of the conversations that I've been having with our nation's spiritual, political, and educational leaders would be occurring today if I hadn't had the excuse of hunting to be silent when I was in high school. For it was in the silence of nature that I first began hearing the answer to the question, "Who am I?"

Opportunity

First and foremost—get quiet! This is the greatest gift you can give yourself. If possible, go away on a silent retreat for a week or weekend. It can be as simple as going backpacking for two days or renting a cabin without a television or radio. If you're not able to get away then take a meditation course.

Meditation is one of the simplest, yet most powerful ways to immerse yourself in silence. The local paper or natural food store bulletin board is a good place to look for meditation classes being offered in your area.

Secondly, get into nature. Take a walk in the park or the woods. Drive to the desert, the ocean, the mountains, the prairie, or a river and simply absorb it. Leave your to-do list (and cell phone) at home and allow yourself time just to unwind in nature. I've found activities like hiking, snowshoeing, cross-country skiing, fishing, photography, and backpacking to be wonderful for this purpose. Check to see if your town or city has any outdoor activity clubs. Often these are wonderful ways to be introduced to new trails and getaways which are within an hour or two of your home. As you venture out keep in mind what Albert Einstein said, "Look deep into nature, and then you will understand everything better."

---

more from nathan...

last read: being peace by thich nhat hahn

what people don't understand about our generation: we have the potential to make a real difference. we have the ability to educate ourselves more fully about a wider range of issues than any generation before us. we are at a critical point in the history of our nation and modern civilization. our generation has in its power the ability to determine what sort of future beings will have on this planet.

life motto: i'm not sure who i am, but i know who i've been. -modest mouse

read more of what nathan had to share in "how can i quit procrastinating?"

nathan radzak, 26

hometown: twig, mn

favorite movie: braveheart

biggest concern: poverty and war (or any type of violence)

favorite book: the world according to garp by john irving

what you wish you knew two years ago: the journey is more important than the destination

life motto: every man dies, but not every man really lives.

madeline radzak, 23

hometown: colorado springs, co

this summer: got married

biggest concern: making sure both my husband and myself are happy and fulfilled

last concert: beastie boys this past friday

favorite food: any fruit

worst date advice: take him home the first night

what you wish you knew two years ago: that i would fall in love with a great man and get married!

life motto: ride it big and tall or not at all (my husband gave me crap about this)

read more of what madeline and nathan had to share in "when should i marry?"

48

CHAPTER EIGHT

How can I overcome this empty pit feeling inside?

"It was the most pathetic moment of my life. I had reached the top, but it was empty," Sarah, age 20, told me.

Sarah should have been the happiest girl in the stadium, after all, dancing had been her life long dream. Now in college she was a member of the University of Colorado's Gold Rush Dance Team, an elite group of 12 girls that performed at football games in front of sold out crowds. On top of her form, Sarah found herself in the middle of 65 thousand fans as the University of Colorado faced the University of Texas in Dallas. Six years of practice and hard work had finally landed her in the same arena where the Dallas Cowboy cheerleaders became famous. But instead of the game being a dream come true, it became a nightmare.

"It was cold, raining, and absolutely miserable," Sarah told me. "I was dancing in front of a sold out crowd when I noticed one of the cameras for national television right on me. At the same time, someone was taking a picture of me from the side. Suddenly, I realized that I'd spent six years of my life trying to earn my way to this point and it meant nothing. These people at home watching television weren't going to care who I was. The TV camera guy didn't care who I was. Nobody cared who I *really* was. They just wanted a picture for right then. I was completely miserable and crying in the picture because I was so cold, and I still had to smile because the camera was on me."

patricia s. prenger, 21

favorite food: anything chocolate

biggest concern: how to pay for graduate school

secret to life: if i knew, i wouldn't be here filling this out!

final thought: your 20s are like a second adolescence. it's a renewed time of figuring out who you are and what you want to be as you move into the next phase of your life.

This marked the beginning of a new life for Sarah. Two years after the Texas game, she left college and joined the Community of the Beatitudes, a Catholic community located in Denver, Colorado, where she's currently studying to become a nun. "People don't understand at all. They think, 'Oh, you threw away all those fun years.' But what did I throw away? I threw away a lot of superficiality, a lot of emptiness. Becoming a nun is not an easy life. But it's a beautiful life."

When the glitter and glitz of dancing and performing in the spotlight lost their meaning, Sarah lost her feelings of enjoyment and excitement. Just like the old expression says: She'd climbed the ladder of success, only to discover it was leaning against the wrong wall.

Every day, you and I are bombarded with messages about how we can become happier, hipper, and more popular: "Use *this* toothpaste and a hot girl or guy will fall for you." "Drive *this* car and your neighbors will envy you." "Wear *these* clothes and your boss will promote you." "Earn *this* salary and happiness will follow." "Go to *this* school and you'll be successful." "Marry *this* person and you'll be living the American Dream." "Eat *this* food and the perfect body will result." Says who? Companies trying to sell us their products pump most of these messages at us. They lead us to believe that power (a new SUV or truck), fortune (lottery tickets or wealth building infomercials), and fame (a brand of shoes worn by Lebron James) are the keys to a good life.

If that were so, then Callie Rogers, 16, from England, should be one happy girl after winning 1.9 million pounds in a lottery jackpot. Despite having all that money can buy she admits to "not having a happy moment" since she was awarded the prize. "Two months ago, I thought I was the luckiest teenager in Great Britain," said Callie. "But today I can honestly say I've never felt so miserable."

Callie was rich, Sarah was a dance star, and yet both of them felt empty and alone. Gary Zukav, a regular guest expert on *Oprah* and author of *The Seat of the Soul*,

told me that this kind of emptiness is something he frequently sees in people who are fertile for a change. "The common experience is powerlessness, not belonging, not being able to contribute, not feeling a part of the universe," Zukav said. "It is excruciating. There are two ways you can deal with it. One is to reach outward and try to rearrange the things outside of you: get more money, get a fancier car, get a more attractive partner, get a different haircut, and get a new tee-shirt . . . The other way is to look inward and find the roots of your pain, and then change them with your will. That is the pursuit of authentic power."

Perhaps you have felt a similar sense of emptiness and had to make a choice. I remember in high school, after winning yet another of many tennis tournaments, I was depressed. It made no sense to me. I'd just won. Why wasn't I jumping up and down? Then I understood. Winning a tennis match no longer fulfilled me. I could try to milk my victory for all it was worth, but in reality I could no longer fool myself. While I enjoyed tennis, it was no

thomas rogers, 22

favorite movie:
saturday night
fever

biggest concern:
going back to
prison

best date advice:
be charismatic,
funny, and smooth

favorite song: my
boo by usher

life motto:
whatever it takes

longer an activity that fulfilled my soul. Therefore, I began looking for new activities that brought fulfillment and meaning.

In what areas of your life have you felt emptiness? Maybe going to the bar every Friday night is no longer fun. Or perhaps you are sick and tired of getting involved in roller coaster relationships. Both of these activities have lost their bite. It doesn't mean that they're wrong or that you were foolish for having pursued them. It simply means that the things you used to do no longer work for the person you are becoming. This is a critical time where you can choose to pursue new projects that have meaning to you, or you can continue doing what is comfortable and familiar even if it no longer has any significance or value.

One secret for transitioning into a new way of being is to cultivate a big picture view of the world. **When you are able to see yourself as a part of something much larger than yourself, it fills you up with a feeling of importance.** A woman who is washing the floor of a building because a judge ordered her to do community service is going to have a different experience from a woman who sees washing the floor as an act of service to God. It is the same physical action, yet a completely different motive for the two women. Likewise when you feel that your life matters and that you're here for a reason, you'll make choices which reflect this respect for your life and its potential. You'll willingly explore new activities rather than continuing to feel empty from milking the same activities that are no longer working in your life.

Opportunity

The ability to see the grand mural of life, while performing your individual part in the whole mosaic, is the key to overcoming a feeling of emptiness. How can you feel a void when you see yourself as an important piece of life's artistry? Below are four activities I recommend for cultivating a big picture perspective in your life.

1. Watch the stars on a clear night and reflect on the vastness of the universe. You are sitting on a planet, Earth, which is one of nine planets in our solar system, which is one of a vast number of solar systems in the Milky Way, which is one of 30 billion galaxies in our universe! Is it not a miracle that you and I are here? Haven't you been born at this time and place for a reason? (If you are in New York, NY take the time to go to the planetarium at the Museum of Natural History. I did it seven years ago and still feel the profound impact from the experience.)

2. Watch the movie *It's a Wonderful Life*, where the main character experiences what life would be like if he hadn't been born. Then looking at your life, ask yourself the following:

Who have I made smile and laugh because I am here on Earth?

Who have I helped inspire and motivate because I am here on Earth?

How has my life made a difference, big or small, on this Earth?

leslie schnabel, 22

favorite food:
ice cream

biggest concern:
what job can
i do that will
make me happy
and actually be
productive

best date advice:
make sure you
experience lots
of different
situations with
the person,
so you can see
how they deal
with and react
to things that
aren't in their
comfort zone.

favorite movie:
chicago

3.   Contemplate the miraculous process that two cells, a sperm and an egg, go through in nine months to create you, a baby ready for birth. You can check out a book on embryology at the library to study this. The process will amaze you. Think about the millions of steps that had to occur in those nine months for you to be here today. Isn't just the fact that you exist a miracle?

4. Hike and explore nature. Great places include the Big Sur coastline, the Black Hills, the Appalachian Mountains, the Grand Canyon, Arches National Park, the Redwood Forest, the Rocky Mountains, the North Shore of Lake Michigan, and the Sierra Nevada Mountains. Think about the fact that these natural landmarks have been here for thousands of years before you were born and will be here long after you are gone. Imagine if the trees and mountains could tell you what they have seen over the centuries. What would they say about those who came before you? What will they say about you? Remember, this

is your time. You are the one who gets to participate in life today.

5. Read the book *Quantum Healing* by Deepak Chopra. It may change your perspective on life. It did for me!

Any one of the activities above will help you realize the significance of your life. As Denis Waitley, former Chairman of Psychology with the US Olympic Committee, says, "Winners have the ability to step back from the canvas of their lives like an artist gaining perspective. They make their lives a work of art—an individual masterpiece."

Always remember just the fact that you are here means you've been chosen and that your life matters.

more from leslie...

favorite song: wish you were here by pink floyd

worst date advice: date someone who doesn't have any goals

what you wish you knew two years ago: that i needed more time to get to know myself

next adventure: i'm getting married this summer in europe

life motto: find what makes you happy and try to do it as much as possible

nancy meyers, 27

hometown:
new york, ny

favorite food:
chocolate

biggest concern:
the future

last read: 1984

what you wish you knew two years ago: that i'd want to go to graduate school

secret to life:
if only i knew

career: what career? i'm still trying to figure that out. who knows what i'll end up doing.

life motto: one step at a time

final thought: my generation has been seen as the slackers—a generation not as committed to one career and one job as previous generations. i think all this is true; we are taking longer to find our direction than our parents did. however, i think my generation is suddenly shifting from being the anchorless, clueless, slacker generation to the generation that is newly stepping out into a world of complete uncertainty. we can't get jobs, most of us have no health insurance, and the world is all of a sudden a very unfriendly place. during its formative years, my generation has quickly gone from the aimless slackers that saw life as a buffet table set out for their sampling and enjoyment, to a group of young people caught in the middle of a harrowing and uncertain time period. i think we are about to grow up very fast.

[CHAPTER NINE]

How do I make these major life decisions?

Detective Fred Mock made a good decision while David Headrick made a poor one. David, 19, was caught dumping 18,000 pennies ($180 worth!) into a coin counting machine at a local grocery store in Elkhart, Indiana. Those pennies were taken less than 48 hours earlier from an 88-year-old man during a robbery in which the elderly man was punched in the head and tied up with a phone cord. Police knew that the robber had made away with a lot of change, so when David went to use the local coin counter Detective Mock was waiting for him. In an Associated Press article, the detective reported, "I got to thinking, if I was a person who did this I'd want to convert this to currency as quickly as possible."

David actually made two unwise decisions. First was the robbery and the second was taking the pennies he stole to the local supermarket. His behavior certainly deserves to be nominated for the Stupidest Criminal award.

While David's mistakes are obvious, the decisions you're facing at this time in your life are undoubtedly more challenging. "Do I take the first job that comes along?" "When should I have children?" "How do I know if he/she is the right one for me?" In addition to the stress of facing all of these questions at the same time, there's the pressure of wanting to start out life in the real world on the right foot. You may feel concerned about creating a domino effect where one wrong decision will lead

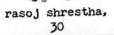

rasoj shrestha, 30

hometown:
dharan, nepal

favorite movie:
terminator i, ii, and iii

biggest concern:
what if i don't have a relationship?

best date advice:
slow and smooth

what you wish you knew two years ago: the powerball numbers

life motto: don't worry, be happy

to another and another until, soon, you'll be so far in a hole that you can't recover.

John, 28, feels this way about his career. Back in college for the second time, he is pursuing a new career in photography, but is concerned about job openings when he graduates. "I think about it all the time," John told me. "Is my degree actually going to pan out? With all the time, energy and money I've put forward, are these things going to benefit me? You hear all these stories about people who went to school and still don't have jobs in their field. I wonder did I make the right decision? It's kind of scary, you know."

Jay Edward Russo, a professor at Cornell University and author of *Winning Decisions,* offered me good advice. He explained that three factors come into play with any decision. First is the decision itself, second is acting on that decision, and third is the role of chance or luck in the outcome. Russo shared the following scenario with me. "Imagine you have 2 pennies in front of you that are biased.

Coin number 1 has a 55 percent probability of turning up heads. Coin number 2 has a 45 percent probability of yielding heads. The coin you select will be flipped only once. If the head appears, you get $10,000 tax-free! If the tail turns up, you get nothing.

"Playing the odds, you choose coin number 1. It's flipped . . . and lands tails up. You get no money. Now, the question is: 'Did you make the right decision?' . . . Yes, because you made the best decision based on your understanding, and you acted on that decision (flipping the coin). However, the third factor, chance, was not in your favor. If you were given another chance to flip the coin for $10,000, which coin would you choose? Again, the best decision would be coin number 1, but it wouldn't guarantee that you'd be right."

Russo explained that we can choose to evaluate the quality of our decisions based on the *process* we use to make them, or on the *result* they obtain. For example, a friend and I wanted to climb Mt. Grey, a 14,000-foot peak in Colorado. The climb

itself is not that technical, except that on the day we chose to climb a blizzard was raging. Add to that, the fact that we weren't prepared—having brought no food, little water, and less than adequate equipment. Even with all of these challenges and our lack of experience on the mountain, we made the decision to attempt the summit anyway. The climb was miserable, but we made it to the top. That evening, when we returned to the truck, our hands and feet were numb and our clothes soaked. We were lucky we didn't get any frostbite.

That day, I was pretty proud of our accomplishment. I thought we'd made a good decision because we made it to the top. In truth, the decision was poor. We foolishly risked getting lost or incurring frostbite, injury, and even death. Simply because the result was favorable doesn't mean the decision was a good one. Likewise, just because a result was unfavorable doesn't mean the decision was a bad one. Remember the penny? Taking a 55 percent shot at coming up

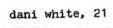

dani white, 21

favorite movie:
empire records

biggest concern:
school and the
health of the
people i care
about

**what you wish you
knew two years
ago:** nothing,
because you can't
really depend on
knowing things
that you don't
know

life motto: dream
as if you'll live
forever. live
as if you'll die
today- james dean

read more of what
dani had to share
in "can i be in
a relationship
and still be
successful?"

heads is always a better choice than a 45 percent shot.

The only fair way to rate your decisions is to evaluate how you arrived at them and to consider the actions you subsequently took. You can control both of these elements, whereas you cannot control chance. As Russo told me, "The best hope for a good decision outcome is a good decision process."

Antoine Yates, 31, a resident of New York City, could have used this advice. After being hospitalized for severe bite wounds, it was discovered that he was keeping a 425-pound tiger and a 5-foot long alligator in his Manhattan apartment! Can you imagine what it would be like if your neighbor across the hall had these two *pets*? Evidently, Antoine was trying to create his own Garden of Eden and made the decision to raise the tiger ever since it was a six-week-old cub. The tiger got so big he had to keep it in a separate room and threw in whole chickens to feed it. Antoine obviously didn't have a good decision making process, and now he faces reckless endangerment charges after he gets out of the hospital.

What is a good decision making process? Debbie Ford, author of *The Right Questions,* taught me that the decisions we make depend on the questions we ask. "Jason, until we ask the right questions," she said, "we can't possibly get the right answers." I agree with Ford. The questions we ask focus our attention on particular areas. For example, when I was looking for a new vehicle I asked many questions. *Which is the best value for the price? What will make me look the best? Which vehicle could I use to haul my gear? What will allow me to get around in the winter? What gets the best miles per gallon? Which will have the greatest resale value?*

Now, depending on which of these questions I place the most importance, I would end up getting entirely different vehicles. If I were going for image, I'd buy a sports car. If room and storage were most important, I'd buy a minivan. If environmental concerns were most important, I'd buy a hybrid of electric and gas. In the end, I decided on an all-wheel drive Toyota Highlander that is fuel-efficient and offers plenty of storage. I also like the way it looks!

So, another key to making good decisions is first to ask yourself all the questions possible and then decide which ones are most important to you. Ford told me, "The truth will set you free, but while most of us say we want one thing, our actions go in another direction." Once you're clear about what is most important, then you can take the appropriate actions that support your decision.

Opportunity

At the top of a sheet of paper, write down the problem for which you need to make a decision. Next, write out all of the questions about the problem. For example:

Problem

Which job should I take?

Questions

How much travel is involved?

What city do I want to live in?

What other opportunities are available?

spud, 20

hometown:
chicago, il

occcupation:
student/cook at
a vegetarian
restaurant

favorite song:
next time by
misery

biggest concern:
the future,
starvation, and
homelessness

last read: a
people's history
of the united
states by howard
zinn

**worse date
advice:** be me!

secret to life:
procreation and
parties

With whom will I be working?

What will my job description be?

Is there room to be promoted?

What can I learn from this job?

Are there benefits?

*Did the previous employee like the
job?*

How far is the commute?

*Will I have evenings and weekends to
spend with my family?*

And so on . . .

You'll discover that once you start asking questions you can go on and on and on. This is good. Keep writing out all the questions you have regarding your problem.

The second step is to go through the questions you want answered and prioritize the top seven. Consider how each of the possible solutions (in this case, which job you may take) answers those top seven questions. Make your ultimate decision based on which solution will best meet your top seven questions.

The third step is to take action on your decision. A decision without action is of little value. After you've taken action you'll then be ready to evaluate the outcome: Was it favorable or not? Did you ask the right questions or not? Did chance ruin the outcome or not? Reviewing decisions later on is a fantastic way to learn from each decision you make. As you fine tune your decision making process by asking better questions and taking more definitive action, you'll soon find that your decisions have better outcomes and you'll become a more confident decision maker.

more from spud...

favorite food: pastas, veggies, tacos—i'll eat it all

what i did last summer: hopped trains across the mid-west from cheyenne, wy, to chicago, il, and then hitchhiked to baltimore, md, and philadelphia, pa.

-saw a guy roll his car on i-80... kicked out his window and dragged him to safety.

-played in a band called the pizza crusties.

-now i work in a killer vegetarian restaurant and i couldn't be happier.

procreation and parties....

kelli ewert, 29

hometown:
creston, ia

favorite food:
corn on the cob

biggest concern:
what the world
will be like as
my kids grow up
in it

favorite book:
summer sisters

best date advice:
meet as many
people as you
can.

life motto:
"the reason why
birds fly and we
can't is simply
that they have
perfect faith."
i saw this on
a friend's dorm
room wall years
ago.

chris ewert, 28

favorite food:
steak

biggest concern:
taking care of my
family

last read: davinci
code

secret to life:
work hard

**difference between
our generation and
our parents:** we
think we can't
live without a
51" tv or a 2
week vacation
to mexico. our
parents never
dreamed of doing
that. we need to
learn how to save
our money.

read more of what
chris had to share
in "where should i
invest my money?"

CHAPTER TEN

Does anyone have it all figured out?

At my college graduation, I remember looking at classmates who knew exactly what they were going to do next and wondering to myself *Why don't I have it all figured out like them?* While I felt confused and uncertain, they appeared confident and sure about the direction of their future. I was envious when these friends started getting married, committed to 30-year mortgages, and began families. *What do they know that I don't?* I'd turn over in my head each night before falling asleep. It irked me that I wasn't ready to make those same choices, and I admired their seeming maturity. But now, only a few years later, many of their confident struts seem instead to be death marches, as they return day after day to jobs they can't stand and relationships that no longer work. Several of their marriages have sadly ended in divorce with the houses being sold and the children splitting time between parents.

Can you think of people, who, like my classmates, seemed to have it all figured out and then their worlds fell apart? Sure. We all can. It's a common story. You can't always judge a book by its cover. Just because someone appears to have it together doesn't mean they really do. In fact, it usually means they don't. That's why we shouldn't judge ourselves in comparison to others. Eddie Cohen, DC, a consultant for Ward Success Systems helped me learn this valuable lesson.

Once, Cohen and I were discussing professional speakers who motivate, inspire, educate,

risa white, 19

favorite food:
candy

biggest concern:
where the united
states is going

favorite movie:
mary poppins

best date advice:
never shut
someone down
right away

**what you wish you
knew two years
ago:** friends and
business don't
mix

life motto: just
keep swimming

and address thousands of people at a time while on stage. Cohen confided in me that while many of the speakers are good within their areas of expertise, behind the scenes some are miserable human beings. On stage, they shine like stars, but when it comes to family life, church participation, or friendships they fall way short of the mark.

Cohen's comment hit me like a stack of bricks dropped from the fourth floor. I had been under the delusion that because someone is good at one activity he or she would automatically be good at every activity. You and I don't have to look far to find evidence to refute this notion. Bill Clinton may be skilled at connecting and influencing people, yet he made momentous errors in his marriage. Whitney Houston may be a talented singer, but she certainly has problems at home and with drugs.

I asked Alison, 29, an intern minister in Tulsa, Oklahoma, if she's had any bad experiences with people she admired. "Yeah, I have. I don't know if I thought they had it all figured out, but I've definitely had heroes—people I looked up to and thought were as near perfect as possible—and then was disappointed by them.

"I feel like that's part of growing up," Alison continued, "realizing that nobody's perfect and realizing that nobody really has it all figured out. At first it can be really disillusioning and then eventually it can be something that gives us hope. We begin to realize, 'Hey, if this person that I really look up to doesn't have it all figured out, then maybe I too have a chance of making a difference in this world.' "

Yes, the bad news is that people can misrepresent themselves. The good news as Alison pointed out is that people have a lot to teach us. Simply because someone is good at golf and horrible at cooking doesn't mean you should ignore him or her. It means you might benefit from listening to what that person says about golf, while it would be wise to take their cooking advice with a grain of salt *or perhaps a lot of sauce*! **The key is to learn from the competencies of others.**

Nancy Cooke de Herrera, a fascinating woman who's considered the meditation teacher to the stars after having taught Lenny Kravitz, Sheryl Crow, Madonna, and Paula Abdul, told me she learned this same lesson while studying with the Indian teacher Maharishi Mahesh Yogi, founder of Transcendental Meditation. Herrera was his assistant in 1969 during the Beatles visit to the Valley of the Saints in India. The Beatles stayed with Maharishi at his ashram for several months, meditating and studying his teachings until John Lennon stormed out in anger following a business mix-up between Maharishi's organization and Apple Corp, the Beatles' company.

When I asked Herrera how Maharishi, a man who was thought to be a saint, could have made such a mistake, Herrera simply told me, "Just because he was a man of God doesn't mean he was a businessman."

Herrera shared great advice. We all have strengths and weaknesses. It's part of being human. I've yet to meet anyone who has it all figured

chad hillje, 22

favorite food:
steak

biggest concern:
what's next in my
life

favorite movie:
napoleon dynamite

**worst date
advice:** if it's
bad, have fun and
make it worse

**what you wish you
knew two years
ago:** she will
break up with me

life motto: it's
not aptitude but
attitude that
determines your
altitude in life

out, but by the same token, I've never met anyone I couldn't learn at least one thing from. As Herrera pointed out, just because someone shines in one area, it doesn't mean they shine in all areas. Learn from the skills and abilities they excel in and let the other areas go.

Who do you know that you can look up to in a particular area? Remember, it doesn't have to be in all areas. Rather, it may be a friend's ability to stick with an exercise program or a co-worker's knack for meeting new people. The key is first to identify the characteristics and skills you want to further develop and then think of people you know who've got that aspect of their lives figured out and study them. The best part is you don't even have to know them. For example, if you wanted to know how Benjamin Franklin managed his time so well, you can read books about the American legend. With the popularity of books and the internet it doesn't matter if the person you want to learn from is alive or dead, you have the ability to learn a great deal from them without ever actually meeting.

Opportunity

No one person has it all figured out, but there's no shortage of people who can teach you valuable lessons in specific areas of life. By following the simple steps below, you will shave months, even years, off your learning curve by focusing on what people do have figured out, instead of what they don't.

1. Make a list of five characteristics and skills you want to master, such as the characteristics of compassion, integrity, and patience; or skills of cooking, golf, and carpentry. It may help you to think of your favorite movie and television characters. What are the characteristics these characters possess that you would like to develop in your life? Perhaps it's the confidence of Morpheus in the *Matrix* or the focus of Erin in *Erin Brokavich*.

2. Pick out as least one person who has mastered the skills for each of the characteristics you wrote down. He or she can be a neighbor,

colleague, coach, or someone whom you can easily research.

3. Study these people thoroughly and ask the following questions:

What is their view of the world?

How do they invest their time?

What do they think about when performing/working?

How do they prepare for each day?

What is their presence like?

How do they carry themselves? walking? sitting? breathing?

How do they dress?

4. Learn everything you can about the skills you want to acquire. Then practice being and performing like the person you want to become.

5. The final step is to integrate your new characteristics into your life. The goal isn't to become someone you're not, but instead to realize you're surrounded by people every day who can help you become more of what you can be.

WHERE ARE YOU FROM

Portland, OR

FAVORITE PLACE TO VISIT

Boston, New York, Italy

age 21

WHERE TO YOU LIVE NOW

Denver, CO

FAVORITE FOOD

? Anything chocolate.

FAVORITE SONG

Right now, "Hey Ya!" by Outkast, but if I'm hon
"Keep on loving you" by REO Speedwagon is up there

BIGGEST CONCERN AS A QUARTERLIFER

How to pay for grad school

LAST BOOK YOU READ

The Rule of Four, Beowulf, The Amazing
Adventures of Kavalier + Clay

FAVORITE MOVIE

Casablanca

BEST DATE ADVICE

Be yourself

WORST DATE ADVICE

Eat Spaghetti & talk about Exes.

SECRET TO LIFE

If I knew, I wouldn't be filling out a survey.

FINAL THOUGHT?

Your 20s are like a second adolescence — it's a
renewed time of figuring out who you are —
what you want to be as you move into the
next phase of your life

CHAPTER ELEVEN

What can I do about all this stress?

"I was just enraged," said Timothy Pilgreen, age 26. "Just so mad and drunk that when they took off, I started following them."

After an argument at the beach, Timothy stole a pick-up truck and began chasing six members of the biker gang known as the Outlaws. He sped-up behind them and one-by-one rammed all six of the bikers, killing two of them. "It was madness," he recalled. "I just closed my eyes, pushed the gas, and blam, blam, blam, just like that."

Now Timothy's full of regret. "I realize I made a mistake," he said. "I know I did something I shouldn't have, and I know I can't take it back. I just wish I could. I'm not a bad person, but I've been so lost and so hopeless for so long."

Timothy felt stressed, lost control of his thoughts and actions, and now he's paying the price. When was the last time you felt close to that breaking point? Have you ever felt like cutting someone off? Have you ever felt like screaming into the phone? Sure we all have. But obviously there are better ways of dealing with stress than running over six bikers.

There's never been a more stressful time in history than right now. Today we have added deadlines, responsibilities, and choices in numbers far exceeding what our ancestors ever dreamed possible. We try to accomplish more in less time and with greater expectations. In fact, did you know that certain preschools in Virginia have eliminated nap-time because

christina kiel, 18

biggest concern: the economy and job outlook

favorite movie: street car named desire

what you wish you knew two years ago: not to make my mother so upset

favorite food: spaghetti

life motto: live everyday to its fullest

they think the 45 minutes are better spent with the 4-year-olds studying than sleeping. One preschool official said, "They can't be babied. These are young minds. We have to take advantage of this early stage when they grasp everything."

So what do we do? The potential for stress is only going to increase as the world continues to speed up. I asked Mary Loverde, former director of the Hypertension Research Center at the University of Colorado School of Medicine and author of *Stop Screaming at the Microwave,* if she thought stress management techniques like prioritizing and time management really worked. "I believe in all those strategies—managing, organizing, delegating, prioritizing, and simplifying," she told me. "They're invaluable. You and I have to have them, but the fact of the matter is that if those things were enough we should be in balance by now. Take time management for example. For every hour that I allegedly save I've got ten hours of demands competing for it.

"They're wonderful strategies but not philosophies of life. What we have to do is come to terms with the fact that we are not going to get it all done. That has been the old life balance model. You make a list you put A, B, C, and if you work it then your life will be in balance. Well, unfortunately, we have now created a world in which we have more things to do than is humanly possible. When you think of prioritizing all the things that are important—your family, career, children, health, community, and spirituality—exactly how do you prioritize all that?"

Loverde brings up a good point. You can't expect to get it all done! In fact, just the belief that it's possible is stressful, because you will get down on yourself when you're not able to finish all your projects.

Samatha, 23, a single mother of a five-year-old daughter knows all about this stress. "There is never enough time left at the end of the day. I wake up, get my daughter ready, fix a quick breakfast, and then we're off. She goes to daycare and I go to work. At the end of the day

I rush back to daycare before they close. Then it's home, dinner, and getting her ready for bed."

She continued, "By the end of the day I don't have any energy left to do the things I know I should—like working out, looking for new career possibilities, or just hanging out with a few friends. I feel guilty about it, but there's nothing I can do about it."

Even though you may not have children, I bet you can relate to Samatha's schedule. Personally, my life changed the day I realized balance in life is not possible. There wasn't enough time in the day to do all the things I wanted to do, so I had to prioritize the activities I did. One *New York Times* bestselling author explained it to me like this, "A balanced life is a myth. What is possible is a life that honors your most treasured priorities and values however you define that as an individual." The author continued, "Believe me, when I am writing a book, that book is a priority. Am I living a perfectly balanced life? Absolutely not! Eighty to ninety percent of my time is spent writing,

anthony wilson, 20

favorite food: pizza

biggest concern: what i'm going to be when i grow up. right now i have an $18,000 degree and still work at starbucks.

best date advice: you're better than what you think you are

what you wish you knew two years ago: nothing...it wouldn't have mattered. i take things as they come.

life motto: it happens

but I am living a life that honors my values and most treasured priorities."

I once read that on average each of us has 30 to 300 hours of catch-up work we just can't seem to find time for. That's a week to a month's worth of backed-up activities. Fortunately there are specific things we can do to reduce stress.

Robert Sapolsky, a professor at Stanford and author of *Why Zebra's Don't Get Ulcers*, told me one of the main areas to focus on is control. "When we feel like we have to control everything that occurs in life it's overwhelming," he said to me. **The key is to control the things you have control over and let go of the things you don't.** You *do* have control over what you focus on as a priority, you *do* have control over how you react to a person, you *do* have control over the when you leave for an appointment, but you *don't* have control over how someone treats you, you *don't* have control over the traffic on the highway, you *don't* have control over the economy. Just acknowledging this can make all the difference.

As Sapolsky says, "In our privileged lives, we are uniquely smart enough to have invented these stressors and uniquely foolish enough to have let them dominate our lives. Surely, we have the potential wisdom to banish their stressful hold."

Opportunity

Two great lessons for dealing with stress are contained within the opening of the Serenity Prayer.

"Lord, grant me the serenity to accept the things I cannot change, courage to change the things I can, and the wisdom to know the difference."

With any stressful event, ask yourself: *Can I change the circumstances that are occurring?* If the answer is yes, then ask *What can I do to make this situation better?* Your responses will provide you with what action you can take if you have the "courage to change the things you can."

The second step is to ask *Even if the circumstances stay the same, can I change the way I'm reacting to the situation?* Events don't cause stress in your life. It's your reaction to events that creates the stress. When you realize this, you will experience the serenity that comes with "accepting the things you cannot change."

Two other recommendations that Sapolsky emphasized to me are to surround yourself with social support and to have outlets for frustration. While basic suggestions, their benefits can't be overstated. People with supportive friends weather the storms of life better. If you're new to an area and don't have any friends, then pay for support if you need it. Go to a psychologist, counselor, or minister and let them be of assistance to you.

Likewise, the best way for our physiology to get rid of a stressor is to work it out. Obviously punching your boss or running over six bikers are not good choices, but exercise is. In fact, it's the greatest constructive outlet for frustration that I know of. Plenty of studies have shown that regular exercise, such as hiking, mountain biking, basketball, tennis,

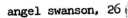

angel swanson, 26

and skiing, significantly reduces stress in people's lives.

By following the wisdom in the Serenity Prayer, finding support, and having constructive outlets for your frustration, you will defuse the drama in your life.

hometown: so many places...my buddies in nyc would say my eight years there don't count, so dallas, tx; rio de janeiro, brazil; monmouth beach, nj; middletown, nj; and mason city, ia

biggest concern: state of this country, the world, and the human spirit... including my own life

motto - stay vigilant!

read more of what angel had to share in "who am i?"

CHAPTER TWELVE

How can I overcome this feeling of being stuck?

Without warning Sherry DeCrow's flashlight flickered and died! She and John Hadar were left stranded in a remote Colorado cave with no food or water. Ironically, the entrance was only 400 feet away, but in the complete darkness they couldn't find their way out. So they just sat and waited.

Outside the cave was anything but stillness. After the couple failed to return home, family members contacted the police. A national missing persons alert was issued, as helicopters and dogs searched the area. When the couple's vehicle was located near the cave, police deputies shouted into the entrance, yet heard no reply. Five days later, family members, conducting a search of their own, went into the cave for the first time. Shortly after entering, their headlamps shown upon the tired faces of Sherry and John. Dehydrated and barely able to utter a whisper, the pair was otherwise in good condition and were safely rescued.

The feeling of being stuck, trapped, and isolated, as though you've wandered into a dark cave, is common as you venture out on your own into the real world. LeighAnn, a 27-year-old in Denver, Colorado, has faced this feeling for several years. "It was mostly that there were so many things I wanted to do, I didn't know where to start," LeighAnn told me. "I wanted to do something that would make my family proud because I was a college graduate, and then I wanted to do acting, then dancing, and then I wanted to live in other places. There

quiney ealy, 19

last read: fallen angels

biggest concern: going to jail or prison

secret to life: don't stress

life motto: the thing you'll die for is the same thing you'll live for

were just so many things I wanted to do that I couldn't pick one. That was the hardest thing—just picking one and going with it." Not sure of what she wanted to do, LeighAnn did what many quarterlifers do—nothing. This is what I call the "deer in the headlights syndrome." Like a wild deer caught in the middle of the road facing oncoming traffic, you don't know which direction to turn and you end up freezing only to get run over by life.

For a deer, the only way to avoid becoming road kill is by moving, and that's exactly what LeighAnn began doing. She knew that she liked entertaining people, so instead of freezing she got involved doing activities she enjoyed. She took an acting class, a writing class, taught dance lessons, tutored a fifth grader, and worked on weekends at special events selling products and drinks, all while holding down a job as a receptionist in a doctor's office. Here's the lesson. Unlike the couple lost in the cave, LeighAnn isn't waiting for someone to rescue her, or for a "big break" to get her unstuck and set her free. Instead, she's taking the steps necessary to prepare, so that when the opportunity presents itself she will be ready to snag it. In the process, she's enjoying herself, making friends, and feels like she is contributing to the lives of others.

William Moreau, a chiropractor who specializes in treating athletes, taught me an important lesson several years ago. "You have to know what you need to know," he said, "before you need to know it." William was referring to providing care at sporting events. "If an athlete injures a knee, ankle, or her neck you had better be prepared to handle it, otherwise you shouldn't be there." When on site you have to act immediately, while keeping the safety of the players in the forefront of your mind. Making a split second decision to pull a player from the game, clearing the field, sending for additional help, treating the injured player on the sidelines, and giving that player permission to return to action all are decisions you must be ready to make. The better prepared you are, the greater the chance of a beneficial outcome. Just like in life. Remember the saying,

"Luck is where opportunity meets preparation."

Actress Roma Downey, who was the lead in the series *Touched by an Angel*, shared a similar insight in an interview I watched recently. "In this business, we are so often waiting for the phone to ring; for the job offer to come in," she said. "The last thing you would want to happen is for the phone call finally to come and for you to find yourself in some way not prepared." For Roma, staying prepared means to exercise, improve upon her acting skills, meditate, eat well, and expand her presentational skills. So, even when she doesn't have a steady job she is continually preparing for a future opportunity.

Just like it's wise for a lumberjack to sharpen his saw before trying to cut down a tree, it's important for you to prepare for your future. Here is the challenge, though. When you're sitting on the ground sharpening the saw, it's easy to feel like you are stuck, as though you're wasting time. There are a lot of quarterlifers who make the mistake of forgetting that preparation is

kecia seyb, 24

hometown:
johnson city, ks

favorite food:
macaroni and cheese

biggest concern:
that i'm not going to find the perfect job

what i did last year: taught english in south korea

favorite movie: gone with the wind

best date advice: be yourself

life motto: if you want to be happy, be

an important part of the process of becoming great and attaining goals. Just because you haven't received a promotion, landed a record contract, finished a book, started a family, or organized a trip doesn't mean you are stuck. As long as you're preparing and practicing, you're moving forward. Interestingly, in my own life, and in the lives of others, I've seen that whenever a new skill or ability is learned an opportunity suddenly comes along to apply it.

When I opened my chiropractic office, Health and Harmony, PC, I began giving talks every other week. I called these classes the Health Education and Awareness Lectures, or H.E.A.L. As the number of people attending the classes increased, I sought out professional help in becoming a better communicator. Within two months, I was noticing significant improvements when suddenly the opportunity arose to expand my message to radio. After several months of hosting a radio show, I once again sought out professional help. Again, I noticed improvements in my communication skills, and shortly thereafter an opportunity arose to spread my message via television as well. Thus, I'm a firm believer that when you prepare yourself for an activity the opportunity for that activity will soon present itself to you.

The key to not feeling stuck is to continue to learn and expand in those areas that are the most interest to you. Check out a book, watch a video, take a course, seek a mentor, do whatever it takes so that you're growing. Remember this adage: When you are green you're growing. When you're ripe, you rot.

Opportunity

As long as you continue to increase your skills and understanding, you'll never be stuck. A friend of mine is fond of saying, "You must study and prepare so that when your day comes you'll be ready." In this information age, you and I are very fortunate to have instant access to resources from around the world. The following are several resources I have found helpful in keeping me from getting stuck.

THE INTERNET

I rejoiced when I first discovered the search engine **www.google.com**. In a matter of seconds you and I have access to information from across the globe just by punching in a keyword. While chances are that you know about **www.google.com** what you may not be familiar with is the newstracker service offered at the site. By clicking on *News* and then on *News Alert* you can enter in the topic that interests you and every day your email account will be sent the latest articles and information about that subject. This is a great way to keep abreast of the latest happenings.

COMMUNITY CLASSES

Chances are that your community center, community college, or local clubs are offering a variety of classes year round. The benefits of these classes are the following:

1. The class size is usually small which allows for more one-on-one instruction.

trent babish, 24

favorite food: mexican

biggest concern: supporting and raising a family ...when that time comes!

favorite book: tuesdays with morrie

worst date advice: follow the hollywood formula in dating—be infatuated with someone, act on that as if it were love, find out it was all wrong, hurt someone, and repeat.

life motto: to live like i'm dying!

2. You meet others in the community who share similar interests as you. These people may become valuable friends and resources as you move forward.

THE LIBRARY

One of the first resources I always turn to when I need to learn a new skill or expand my understanding is the good old public library. I regularly will check out 25 books or more at a time when learning a new skill or topic. You can visit the library online and in a matter of minutes reserve and request books in the area that interests you. If you're not familiar with the library's book search, visit or call a librarian and she will gladly take you through the process. If fact, most libraries now have an "Ask the Librarian" online link that lets you type in a question and the librarian will research it and email back the answer.

PEOPLE

This may be your best resource. Call up professionals and experts in the areas that you're genuinely interested in learning about. As long as you're respectful of their time, most will be flattered to meet and share with you. I have found the following introduction to be an effective way to arrange a first meeting. "Hello, Mrs. Nelson. My name is Jason Steinle. John Lewis gave me your number and recommended that I call you. I've been working on a book (or whatever it is you're interested in talking to them about) and John tells me you have published a book and know a lot about the business. May I speak with you over the phone for five minutes or take you out for lunch some time this week? I'd like to know more about your book."

Give any of these four resources a try and you'll find yourself getting new ideas and moving forward once again. Next time you feel like you are spinning your wheels keep in mind the words of civil rights pioneer, Whitney Young Jr., "It is better to be prepared for an opportunity and not have one, than to have an opportunity and not be prepared."

```
more from trent...

favorite movie: a
river runs through
it

what you'll be
doing in five
years: i will be
happily married
with a young
family (god
willing). as far
as a career goes,
hopefully i will
be finishing up
with great lakes
airlines, and
moving on to
frontier airlines.
i'd also like to
have a small real
estate investing
company going on
the side with my
sister. lastly,
but certainly
not least, i will
be supporting
whatever it is
that my family is
doing at the time
and helping out
with whatever they
may need.

read more of what
trent had to share
in "how can i
overcome my fear
of failure?"
```

live like you're dying...

erin britney head, 26

hometown:
minneapolis, mn

biggest concern:
am i making a
positive impact
in/on my world?

best date advice:
be yourself—
you'll save
everyone a lot of
time

**favorite
book:** the four
agreements by don
m. ruiz

life motto:
the only thing
in your way
of anything is
yourself.

read more of what
erin had to share
in "what is the
meaning of life?"

brandon head, 26

hometown:
baxley, ga

favorite food:
steak

biggest concern:
providing for my
family

favorite movie:
lonesome dove

worst date advice:
take a third
person

favorite book: to
kill a mockingbird

**what you wish you
knew two years
ago:** winning lotto
numbers

life motto: try
not to sweat the
small stuff

CHAPTER THIRTEEN

How can I quit procrastinating?

Maria did not hesitate or stray once from her job. She knew what she had to do and she did it. In fact, it was simply a matter of life or death.

Maria, 49, an employee of Compass Bank, was on her lunch break when a criminal handed her a bag. "If you don't do exactly as I say," whispered the thief, "the bomb in this bag will kill you." With her life literally in her hands, Maria entered the bank at 12:30 P.M. and robbed it. Once outside, she handed the stranger the money and he disappeared. As it turns out the bag did not contain a bomb, Maria lived, and the thief has yet to be captured.

Like Maria, you don't procrastinate when the stakes are high enough. Right now you may be working a job you dislike because the income prevents you from having your car repossessed. On the other hand, I bet there are many activities you are putting off simply because the stakes aren't that significant. If failing to exercise three times a week meant that your house would be foreclosed on, chances are that you'd exercise! But life doesn't work that way. It's more forgiving with some activities than with others. You miss a workout; the sun still comes up the next day. Unfortunately, this is the root of the problem. It's easy to put life off. *I'll get to it tomorrow, I'll have more time at the end of next week,* or *I'll start after the holiday season* are all mantras for the habitual procrastinator.

Brian Tracy, a leading authority on personal effectiveness and author of *Eat That Frog*, told me, "All motivation requires motive. Therefore you have to ask what is

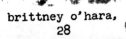

**brittney o'hara,
28**

hometown:
missoula, mt

biggest concern:
exposure to
environmental
toxins

favorite movie:
pretty in pink

best date advice:
don't make
the first move
(woman). wait for
him to call you

**what you wish you
knew two years
ago:** you can't
force someone
else to change
or behave in a
certain way

life motto: love
yourself and
don't lead with
the ego

your motive? Ask yourself, 'What would I love to do with my life if I had no limits—physical, mental, spiritual, or financial?' Set big goals. Unless you have a motive, you can't be motivated." For Maria, her motive was saving her life. For you, it may be your business idea, your children, your sense of adventure, your desire to feel good, and so on.

Nathan, 18, has a clear motive. He wants to be Governor of Colorado and then the President of the United States. In fact, he is so clear about his direction that as a sophomore in high school he requested applications from Harvard, Yale, Stanford, Princeton, and other colleges because he wanted to know exactly what they were looking for in their students. "The summer after my sophomore year was when I first visited several colleges in the Midwest," Nathan told me. "As that year went on I started to look at the admission requirements for some of the upper schools I was going to be shooting for and tried to tailor my high school career to those." Nathan filled his schedule with activities that would help him realize his dream. By the time of his high school graduation, he had been class president, editor of the school newspaper, president of the National Honor Society, captain of the cross-country team, a member of the wrestling team, and class valedictorian. He received college acceptances and scholarships from a dozen schools and in the end decided on Harvard, because it will help move him towards his goals.

Was it easy to be so involved in all of those activities? No. Will Nathan become just as involved at Harvard? You bet! Why? Because he has a compelling reason for doing what he does.

What is your motive in life? What is the impact that you want to have? What is the difference you want to make?

Except for extreme cases, every one of us can lose weight, read a book, make a phone call, submit a résumé, research a town, plan a special date, and learn to play the guitar. The only thing stopping us is our lack of motivation to do these things. When we don't,

it's not really a problem of time constraints, because the truth is that we're always doing something. Even doing nothing is doing something. It's just a matter of acknowledging what the "something" is that we've chosen to do.

During my first year of undergraduate studies, I lived in the dorms. There was always a game of Nintendo or Sega going in one of the rooms. At any time of the day, whether it was two in the afternoon or two in the morning, three to eight guys would be gathered around a television watching the game being played. While the guys in my dorm rarely missed a game, they did miss a lot of their college education. Most of them didn't go to class and certainly didn't turn in their assignments.

Were they procrastinators? That depends on your point of view. They didn't procrastinate on Nintendo tournaments, although they did with their education. It was a matter of motive. The drive to master the video game outweighed the desire to earn a bachelor's degree and begin a career.

87

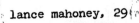

lance mahoney, 29

location:
waukon, ia

favorite food:
ben & jerry's
chocolate chip
cookie

biggest concern:
finances

last read: the
four agreements

**what you know now
you wish you knew
two years ago:** in
business it can
be easy to get
taken advantage
of

**worse date
advice:** talk
about yourself a
lot

life motto:
everything
happens for a
reason

Guess what happened when the second semester came around? Only one of these eight guys in my dorm returned to college. Were the others failures? They were failures according to the school's values and probably according to the values of their parents, but according to their own values they were not. They'd simply placed a greater importance on leisure than on getting an education.

Where they may have failed was in realizing what was truly going to offer them long-term leisure. While the video game playing was fun during that initial semester, a poor education virtually guarantees a lifetime of nine-to-five days with little freedom left in the schedule to play for the next 60 years.

To change behavior, we need to examine and take advantage of our motives. I recently read a newspaper article that captured this idea well. In Durango, Colorado, the United Blood Services was having a hard time getting enough blood donations, so they sweetened the deal. For each pint of blood donated, a person received a pint of beer. Four local breweries donated the beer and the residents donated the blood. The blood drive was a huge success because it gave the people of Durango a motive for donating.

Here is the key to overcoming procrastination. Link your activities with your purpose in life. It may be boring to work the graveyard shift at the convenience store, but if that job is funding production of your future film it becomes an important part of your mission. Associate every activity you do with the big picture of your life. It may be easy to skip a workout if you feel tired tonight. However, it's hard to skip a workout if you remind yourself that each workout prepares you to have the energy, mental clarity, and physical presence necessary to be promoted to vice president of your company.

Opportunity

The easiest way to overcome procrastination is by shedding a new light upon the activity. Below is a simple process you can use to change your perspective from *Do*

I have to do it? to *When do I get to do it?*

Step One:

Write down five tasks that you've been avoiding. Look at each one individually, and then ask yourself the following questions:

> *How will completing this task help me to achieve my dream?*

> *How much time and energy do I lose every day thinking about this task?*

> *What is the cost of not completing this task?*

By answering these three questions, you begin to link the completion of the task with forward momentum toward your goal.

Step Two:

Put the task in proper perspective by asking three more questions. All too often we make a mountain out of a molehill. Once you have answered these questions you should have a more accurate understanding of your situation.

val schettler, 23

hometown:
lemars, ia

last read: boring
college textbooks

biggest concern:
finding the
perfect office
to work in after
graduation

favorite movie:
pay it forward

life motto:
"therefore, do
not worry about
tomorrow, for
tomorrow will
worry about
itself. each
day has enough
trouble of its
own."

—matthew 6:34

*What do I need to do to
complete this task?*

*Realistically, how long will it take
to complete this?*

If I start today, when will I finish?

Step Three:

Take action. One way to increase your chance of success is to recruit others to hold you responsible. Announce to your friends, your spouse, or your co-workers that you intend to finish your task in two days (or however long you've assessed it takes). Ask them to check-up on you at intervals. If you're really serious, build in a checks and balances system. For instance, you might tell them that for each day you go past your deadline you will buy them lunch that day. A few meals at an expensive restaurant may be just the motivation you need! Remember as Pablo Picasso said, "Action is the foundational key to all success."

CHAPTER FOURTEEN

How can I stay motivated?

Charles Marsh will tell you, "I'm an old guy who's happy as a lark." At 81, he must be, or he wouldn't still be practicing medicine. Not only is "Doc" still working when most folks his age are retired or dead, he's also been doctoring patients in the same small town, Drexel, Missouri, since 1948. In fact, he has no plans to retire anytime soon. "There's not too many of us old guys left," says Marsh. "I'll go as long as I can." Doc is a prime example of someone who has kept his motivation strong day after day, month after month, decade after decade.

Can you imagine doing the same job for 55 years? Sara, 27, a friend of mine, lost her motivation after only three years of teaching. "It's the thought of teaching for the next 30 years that's most stressing," she told me. "I got into it because I loved teaching and working with children,

but the politics are ridiculous. It's no longer something I enjoy."

Sara's not alone. Chances are that you're also bored with your career and life. According to research, Americans between the ages of 24 and 32 change jobs every 1.2 years! One of the primary reasons is we expect the grass to be greener on the other side. We think, "This job is dull, monotonous, and painstakingly slow, so hopefully the next one will be exciting, varied, and engaging." Unfortunately, that's not usually the case. Too often, I have seen that it's not the job that's the problem, but rather the uninspired person performing the job.

John Demartini, a long time mentor of mine and author of *Count Your Blessings*, taught me the value of investing in inspiration. He advised me, "Travel whatever distance, pay whatever price,

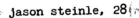

jason steinle, 28

biggest concern: forgetting and becoming comfortably numb

what you wish you knew two years ago: the importance of relationships in all walks of life

favorite movie: dead poets society

life motto: these are the times i am the person

final thought: thank you for reading this book. i look forward to meeting you.

learn more about jason by visiting jasonsteinle. com

and do whatever it takes to be inspired." In a time of recession and a chaotic stock market, I have taken Demartini's words to heart. This is one reason that I like movies so much. Millions of dollars are spent to create two powerful hours of film that you and I can rent for 99¢ at the grocery store. Take one of my favorite films, *Dead Poets Society*. Do you remember it? If not, spend the 99¢. I watch it two times a year just to be reminded of the motto *carpe diem*, Latin for "seize the day."

Songs, books, people, places, quotes, and stories can all be used for motivation. When I was 24, I founded my chiropractic office, Health and Harmony, PC. I had moved to a state and town where no one knew me and I knew no one. As you can imagine, the first six months were challenging. Learning how to run a business, attract clients, provide exceptional care, pay the bills, and meet new friends was overwhelming. What kept me going day-after-day was that I continually fed my body, mind, and soul with inspiration. For example, I used to listen to Travis Tritt's song "It's a

Great Day" every morning before getting out of bed. This was a little step, but the impact it had on my mindset for the day was significant. Instead of dreading the day, I saw it as an opportunity.

Another practice I adopted in those first months involved a weekly telephone call to a friend, Kevin, who had just opened his first business. He and I would hold one other accountable for meeting our goals. At the end of each phone call, we both named three proactive steps we'd take during the coming week. For example, one week I promised to arrange a talk with the local Kiwanis Club, finish my newsletter, and ask for five referrals from current clients. Simply knowing that I would have to answer to Kevin at the end of the week was motive enough to make me follow through on my action steps that week and in the following weeks.

Over the last four years, by virtue of my radio and TV programs, I've been fortunate to rub shoulders with many of the most successful people in our culture. Do you know what I've witnessed in the lives of those who are moving towards their dreams that I see missing in those who aren't? It's systems. **Successful people have created systems or processes in their lives that help them stay motivated.** These processes intentionally ignite their inner drive to get out there and "do it" rather than just waiting for a mood to overcome them.

Jack Canfield, co-author of the mega-successful *Chicken Soup for the Soul* series, is a good example. Even after selling millions of books he continues to write and conduct seminars around the country. I asked him the secret to staying motivated. "To constantly keep yourself awake is the game, whether that's through meditation, reading uplifting books, or listening to motivational cassettes and CDs."

Canfield continued, "Other ways to do it include teaming up with a partner, being part of a mastermind group, or agreeing with a friend you are going to slap each other any time you see the other giving up on his or her dream. The key is to make a list of all the things you want to do. What is your dream? What do

megan wilson, 32

hometown:
greenwich, ct

biggest concern:
not living my
truth

favorite movie:
groundhog's day

best date advice:
confidence is
attractive. love
yourself! enjoy
yourself!

**worst date
advice:** that
there is anything
to fear

life motto: i am
precious, life is
precious, soul is
precious

you want? Then write it down and review it as your dream list. Every week I go through about 150 things I want to accomplish, experience, do, be, and have before I die. Doing this helps keep me moving forward."

Take Demartini's and Canfield's advice to heart. Instead of waiting for a moment of inspiration or motivation to fall upon you by chance, create it by developing a system. This way rather than depending on the circumstances of your job, workouts, or life to keep you motivated, you become proactive. As Oscar Wilde said, "Success is a science; if you have the conditions, you get the result."

Opportunity

One of the keys to staying motivated at a job and in life is to develop a system that you can use over and over to help get you fired up, focused, and on track. On the following page is a method for developing your own proactive system.

Staying motivated

Step One

The first step is to ensure that you are getting enough of the basics. Your system can't last if you're not covering these basics.

1. Sleep—How many hours of sleep have you had in the last two days?

2. Water—Are you dehydrated?

3. Exercise—Are you moving and stretching your body?

When you have the basics covered, then you are ready to tap into your proactive system.

Step Two

1. Write down the titles of three movies that inspire you.

2. Write down the titles of three songs that inspire you.

3. Write down the names of three people in your life who you know personally that inspire you.

P.S. For a list of recommended movies and songs go to:

www.UploadExperience.com.

Step Three

The next time you're feeling low on motivation, listen to those songs, watch one of those movies, and/or call up one of the people on your list. This is an empowering way to stay motivated. By doing this consistently you will notice a renewed fire of motivation being lit inside of you.

AGE 21

HOMETOWN Rhinelander, WI

WHERE YOU LIVE NOW Denver, CO

FAVORITE FOOD
~~Cheese~~ Mashed potatoes

BIGGEST CONCERN
Finishing school strong

FAVORITE MOVIE
13 going on 30

BEST DATE ADVICE
Be yourself, don't try to hard to impress.

WORST DATE ADVICE
Let her pay

LIFE MOTTO
You haven't Lived until you're ~~tota~~ totaled 3c

WHAT YOU WISH YOU WOULD HAVE KNOWN TWO YEARS AGO
You have to pay back your credit cards

FAVORITE ~~MOVIE~~ SONG
Dobie Gray

~~I want to rest~~ "Drift away"

CHAPTER FIFTEEN

How can I overcome my fear of failure?

The Chicago Bulls created a legacy when they won six of eight NBA championships from 1991-98. Michael Jordan, considered one of the greatest players of all time, was the driving force behind these wins. In fact, the only two years the Bulls did not win the championship were while Jordan was on a hiatus playing baseball. What made Jordan so great? Why did former Boston Celtic Larry Bird say, "I think he's God disguised as Michael Jordan"? It was because of his willingness to fail in order to succeed.

Jordan, himself, said, "I never looked at the consequences of missing a big shot. I can accept failure, but I can't accept not trying." He reached legendary status and became the most decorated player in the NBA because he took the buzzer shots that won or lost the game. He stepped up to the challenge time and time again and was willing to risk it all. As one of Art Thiel's articles on NBA.com says, "The last image of Jordan's on-court career—a game-winning 20-foot jumper in Salt Lake City's Delta Center in June, 1998, to beat the Jazz for the Bulls' final Jordan-era championship—was a repeat of so many devastating knockout punches that it seemed he had been doing these feats forever." Michael Jordan won the hearts of his fans because he was able to overcome his fear of failure on the court.

While few of us will ever suit up for an NBA game, the fear of failure exists in all of our lives. This is especially true in our 20s when we enter the real world and for the first

carrie kubesa, 31

favorite food:
honey nut
cheerios

biggest concern:
that i will
work my child's
childhood away

favorite movie:
the power of one

**what you wish you
knew two years
ago:** how much i
should enjoy the
first five years
of my child's
life

favorite band:
matchbox twenty

life motto: seize
the day

time stand on our own two feet. Like a baby bird pushed from the nest and forced to fly, we wonder, "Will I fly or fall?" We fear falling flat on our face at our job, marriage, finances, and life in general. This is perfectly normal. Everyone that I have spoken with has some level of fear. We get uneasy around the possibility of not succeeding. This uneasiness is enough to paralyze people and prevent them from moving forward. For others, like Jordan, they feed off of it and use it to propel themselves to new heights.

Gary Larson, creator of the *Far Side* cartoon, experienced this fear of failure. In an interview on National Public Radio he shared how he nearly abandoned his career. "I didn't know where my ideas were going to come from. I didn't know if I could do it year after year, or even week after week. I was terrified. I was writing just a weekly cartoon and having a hard time keeping up with that."

Larson overcame his hesitation and took on the challenge of creating a daily cartoon. "When I started, I just wanted to pay the rent. That was my fantasy. Could I actually do something I loved to do and make a living at it? When it reached that level I was completely satisfied."

By overcoming his fear of failure not only did Larson pay the rent, he went on to become one of the wealthiest cartoonists ever!

As a child I was told, "The finest steel comes from the hottest furnace." It seems that in life great pursuits require great risks. Larson risked the security of his home and lifestyle to pursue a career as a cartoonist. Jordan risked losing a championship with his final shot. Christopher Columbus risked falling off the end of the world in pursuit of new lands. Rosa Parks risked abuse to take a stand for what was right. Trent, age 24, risked losing everything as he fought for his life.

At age 20, Trent was diagnosed with a form of cancer known as Hodgkins lymphoma. The cancer went into remission following six weeks of chemotherapy, but returned soon after. I asked Trent how he dealt with the possibility of failing to beat cancer. "I didn't let it be an option in my mind," he said. "In the very beginning I did. When I first heard the news I was pretty let down inside and thought that was it. I tried to keep positive and always look for the next day and hope and pray that the next scan showed positive results. It was obviously a roller coaster ride. After finishing chemotherapy and no cancer showed up, I was like, 'Yes!' And then it shows up again and I was down at the bottom again."

"Your options become less and less," Trent continued explaining. "When chemotherapy fails, then it's radiation, and if the radiation fails, you're looking at a bone marrow transplant. I was always under the assumption that everything was going to be okay. I don't think that I let the failure of the treatments affect me. I tried to be the most positive person about it, but I did have my hard times where I would break down especially to my mom. I didn't try to cover anything up.

ryan pierce, 23

favorite food:
pizza

biggest concern:
war

last read: the
catcher in the
rye

favorite band:
phish

best date advice:
play it cool on
the first date

favorite movie:
napoleon dynamite

life motto:
emancipate
yourselves
from mental
slavery...none
but yourself can
free your mind

Fortunately my mom and my whole town were a huge support."

Trent didn't let cancer shut down his life. Not only did he fight for his life, Trent also took charge. He began leading a youth group in his community. He became more involved in his church and found himself becoming much less judgmental of people. An important point to highlight about Trent is that he kept a balanced perspective. While he wanted to stay optimistic, he also looked at what would happen if the chemotherapy and radiation failed. With this balanced view, Trent was able to overcome his fear of death and move forward with his life. Today his cancer is in complete remission and he is happily pursuing his dream of becoming an airline pilot.

Willie Jolley, author of *A Setback Is a Setup for a Comeback*, recommends looking at the big picture when it comes to fears. "You have to overcome your fears or your fears will overcome you," Jolley told me. "How do you overcome your fears? One, you identify the fact that there is a fear. Two, start taking action. I always give people four questions that will make a critical difference in life. Question number one. 'What's the best that can happen?' Question number two. 'What's the worst that can happen?' Question number three. 'What's the most likely thing that will happen?' Question number four. 'Am I willing to live the worst to get to the best?' If the answer is no then you stay where you are at."

Jolley applied these four questions to his life when he was in his 20s. After being named Washington, DC's top nightclub singer, he unexpectedly found himself out of a job and replaced by a karaoke machine. Jolley had to decide whether to take another job singing in a club or to venture out on his own. "I had to make a decision when I started my company as a speaker. I had only two hundred dollars to my name and two kids in private school," said Jolley. "I asked myself, 'What's the worst that can happen?' Losing my house. I then asked myself, 'What's the best that can happen?' I become massively successful. 'What's most

likely to happen?' I'll earn some money and I'll survive. Then I asked, 'Am I willing to live with the worst, losing my home, in order to get to the best, becoming massively successful?' I said to myself, 'Hmm, I can live with that.'"

Like Jordan, Larson, Trent, and Jolley, everyone I've met who's achieved greatness did so by overcoming their fears. They would rather fail trying than to live with the feeling of never having tried. **In fact, if there's one lesson I've learned in the difference between people who are paralyzed by fear and those who step up and face fear, it's that the latter realize the significance of life and are willing to risk hardship and failure to have a shot at their dreams.** They truly live by the statement, "Nothing ventured, nothing gained."

Opportunity

A practical way to overcome the fear of failure is by putting it into its proper perspective. Often those things we fear are really not as bad as we think, but we let a molehill escalate and build in our minds into

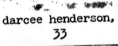

darcee henderson, 33

hometown:
waseca, mn

favorite food:
cheese and café breves!

what you wish you knew two years ago: that life is a wave—go with it and trust it.

biggest concern:
my biggest concern is to lose my health. as long as i have my health i have everything. working as a nurse, i see so many people with irreversible health problems and every day i'm able to count my blessings.

a serious mountain of a fear. As Franklin D. Roosevelt said, "All you have to fear is fear itself."

The next time you face a fearful situation begin by asking yourself the four questions Jolley outlined above. The great benefit of looking at a fear with this perspective is that you immediately can make a conscious decision. Is it worth risking the worst outcome to achieve the best possible outcome? If the answer is no, then you move on. There is no sense in wasting your energy thinking about something you're not willing to commit to at this time. If on the other hand the answer is yes, then you must look at the first steps you can take to move towards the best possible outcome.

Write down these steps and make them SMART. They must be "S" specific, "M" measurable, "A" action oriented, "R" realistic, and "T" time limited. Like any achievement, it is going to require work, but if you keep in mind the four questions and make your goals SMART you will be ready to roll up your sleeves and overcome your fear of failure. As you go forward, remember the

Overcoming fear of failure

words Houston Control Center announced in the movie Apollo 13, "Failure is not an option."

more from darcee...

favorite movie: amelie, napoleon dynamite, whale rider, happy gilmore, foreign flicks, funny flicks, there's too many to list!

best date advice: hmmm...i've pretty much been in committed relationships most of my adult life and haven't "dated" per se. i'll let you know the "best date advice" when i find out.

worst date advice: again...don't know. the only advice i can give at all would be to love people deeply and have no regrets if you've loved well and with all your heart. forgive, love, and live without regret.

life motto: go confidently in the direction of your dreams

dustin craft, 28

hometown:
half moon bay, ca

favorite food:
sushi

biggest concern:
understanding the
depth of living
a life of service
and the courage
to follow through
with it.

secret to life:
be of service
whenever you
can and always
choose to show
up with as much
authenticity and
integrity as you
can.

more from dustin...

**what you wish you
knew two years
ago:** that i can
have it all.

**difference between
our generation and
our parents:** it
seems as though
the focal point
of our parents
generation was
one of security
and "perceived"
certainty, while
in our generation
it seems to be
one of freedom &
uncertainty.

worst date advice:
lie. my thought
is that most date
advice is bad
advice. it usually
involves someone
else telling you
how you should be
and act.

life motto:
change...in a
lifetime or an
instant...you
decide

[WOULD YOU LIKE TO BE IN THE NEXT BOOK?]

Yes. Please interview me for the next book. My story is a good fit for the *UPLOAD EXPERIENCE* book on:

- ❏ Starting a business
- ❏ Car buying
- ❏ Spirituality
- ❏ Home buying
- ❏ Weight loss
- ❏ Investing

- ❏ Finding a career
- ❏ Relationships
- ❏ Dating
- ❏ Parenting
- ❏ Golf
- ❏ _____

Send us your information below or do it instantly online at www.UploadExperience.com.

Name: _____

Age: _____ Email: _____

Street Address: _____

City: _____ State: _____

Telephone: _____

Story Summary:

_____

_____

_____

_____

_____

_____

_____

Please mail survey
to the following address:

UPLOAD EXPERIENCE
PO Box 2367
Evergreen, CO 80437

CHAPTER SIXTEEN

Where can I find Mr. or Ms. Right?

"Go to the park with a dog."

"Learn to play golf."

"Bring you sister's kid to the grocery store."

"Join a church."

"Hang out at a sports bar."

Have you tried any of these strategies? These are all pieces of advice that quarterlifers offered for meeting Mr. or Ms. Right.

Turn on the television and it's *The Bachelor, The Bachelorette, Average Joe, Joe Millionaire, Shipmates, The Fifth Wheel, Elimidate,* and *Blind Date.* Go online and you will find Match, eHarmony, and Matchmaker. Chances are that your city has matchmaking businesses like *It's Just Lunch* and *Great Expectations,* as well as speed dating

and a whole host of other singles events. The pursuit for the perfect partner is alive and well! Despite the many opportunities to meet people, however, the question remains: How do you find the right partner?

Of course, this is one topic everyone seems to have an opinion on. Your aunt knows a "perfect girl" for you at church. Your best friend just met a "great guy" at the gym. A co-worker swears by a local matchmaking service. Your brother recommends you go out to bars. A neighbor insists on chatting to strangers at the bookstore. Yes, everyone seems to have his or her own formula for finding the right person.

Interestingly, when I dug deeper into this topic, I discovered one common underlying theme.

alexis anthony, 26

hometown:
hudson, oh

favorite food:
watermelon

biggest concern:
how commitments,
whether they
be financial,
occupational,
or interpersonal
will affect my
future.

**worst date
advice:** make sure
he pays

**what you wish
you knew two
years ago:** i wish
i knew how to
budget my time
better.

life motto:
the early bird
catches the worm

Everyone agreed that the solution to finding the right partner has more to do with who you are as a person than with any place or event. It's been said, "When the student is ready, the teacher appears." Well, it also seems, "When you are ready, Mr. or Ms. Right appears."

"For me it was just finding a good place for myself," Andy, a 29-year-old chiropractor in Wisconsin, who was recently engaged, told me. "When you're in a good place, you do things to keep yourself balanced; and then you run into that special person because you're open to it. If you're out looking for someone I think you rarely find her, because you may be looking too hard. Instead you find someone who, like you, isn't in the right place herself."

"Meeting someone can happen at the coffee shop, bar, bookstore, gym, or a party," continued Andy. "There isn't a correct place or a wrong place. The place is actually yourself. You have to find your own balance, which means having a good hobby and having the things that make you whole. A lot of people want companionship because they think that will make them whole. But if you're not content within yourself then there will never be anybody else that's going to help you with that. There will never be anybody else to fill that. For me, I was in a really good place when I met Sarah. I felt content and I was just doing a lot of hiking, camping, and journaling, and she was doing the same thing. We ended up really hitting it off because of that. We had similar backgrounds."

Andy hit upon two major points. **First, you must be in a good place emotionally if you want to attract the right partner. Secondly, you should pursue your own interests and hobbies instead of trying to fake an interest just to meet someone.**

Quarterlifers often look to relationships to fulfill them. Is it any wonder? From the time we can first roll over we are told stories where the characters "live happily ever after." Do you remember the popularity of broken heart necklaces in grade school? Our girlfriend or boyfriend wore one half of the heart and we wore the other half. Later

we watched *90210, Friends,* and *Sex in the City,* TV programs where the characters were always looking for the right person to make them happy. Eventually we began to believe that we needed to have someone to make us whole. Most of us believe that someone else holds the key to our happiness.

Sasha Cagen, author of *Quirkyalone,* agrees. "In our culture, relationships are presented as a way to rise above the mundane—through romantic love. The problem is that it may never be all that. It may be wonderful, uplifting, and transcendent for a time, but a relationship isn't going to be like that forever. You have to come to a still point in yourself to find what it is that makes you whole." Cagen, like Andy, thinks the surest way to find the right partner is first to discover and enjoy your own company.

Think about it. I know throughout my life, I've always been attracted to people who seemed to have it "going on." They are energetic, happy, and live life with an air of importance. In short,

john d. paul, 27

favorite food: philly cheese steak

biggest concern: my daughter's future

favorite movie: 50 first dates

worst date advice: be desperate

favorite book: brother cadfiel series

life motto: you have to be true to yourself before you can be true to others

they are confident with themselves and their lives. I bet most of us are attracted to people who embody those kinds of qualities. When we are self-confident, it is like a magnet that attracts people to us. Combine that confidence with pursuing activities we enjoy and the odds of meeting Mr. or Ms. Right increase dramatically.

Too often, I have seen quarterlifers lose their identity and flair as they try to morph into someone they aren't. Hanging out at the sports bar or bookstore to find a potential partner is a terrible idea if you don't care a lick about football or haven't read a book since high school. Sure, we hear that opposites attract, but trust me, a relationship won't last if you are pretending to be someone you are not.

Opportunity

The following exercise is a powerful tool for drawing Mr. or Ms. Right into your life. On a piece of paper, write out all of the characteristics and qualities you want in your dream partner. Put each one on a separate line, using as many sheets of paper as you need. Your list may include adjectives such as adventurous, caring, sexy, witty, authentic, intelligent, and so on. You will find this easy to do. In fact, most people think it is fun.

The second step is a little more challenging. Read your list of ideal partner qualities and for each one ask *Do I possess and exemplify this same quality in my own life?* If the answer is yes, move on to the next item. However, if you answer no, then ask *Who do I need to become to deserve this type of person?*

This is the BIG question and it's important that you understand its essence. *Who do I need to become?* is not the same as *What do I need to accomplish or get?* If you want to connect with a loving person, for instance, you had better be a loving person. It does not mean to go out and buy a diamond necklace and two dozen roses. While giving gifts can be an expression of love, material goods are not a substitute for genuine caring, affection, and understanding.

Likewise if you demand an adventurous person, you need to be adventurous. It doesn't mean run out and purchase a new Northface jacket and Asolo boots. so you can *appear* adventurous.

Finding Mr. or Ms. Right has little to do with location or event, and it has everything to do with you. The bookstore, coffee shop, internet, bar, hiking trail, concert hall, park, theater, church, gym, and grocery store may all be great places to meet people, but the key ingredient is self-esteem. Before you can hope to find the right person, you need to be content with yourself. Experts and quarterlifers seem to agree. Nothing helps attract the right person better than knowing who you are and what you want.

As you go through the list of qualities you'd like to find in your ideal mate, honestly ask yourself to what degree do you possess that same quality. If you don't possess it, you must look for ways to bring out that quality.

leighann gould, 27

favorite food:
ice cream and
strawberries

biggest concern:
am i making the
right decision

best date advice:
don't rush into
anything, see
if you can enjoy
each other as
friends first.
and always say
thank you.

life motto: life
is short, do all
you can while you
can.

read more of what
leighann had to
share in "how can
i overcome this
feeling of being
stuck?"

Here are a few suggestions for appealing qualities:

If you want to be calm, meditate.

If you want to be energetic, work out.

*If you want to be more loving, read books like Gerald Jampolsky's **Love is Letting Go of Fear** and practice the exercises he suggests.*

*If you want to be adventurous, study the lives of adventurous people. **Into the Wild** by Jon Krakauer is a great book to start with.*

As you become more of who you can be the Universe has a mysterious way of attracting Mr. or Ms. Right into your life.

CHAPTER SEVENTEEN]

Am I with the right one?

Silky, smooth sounds of Luther VanDross echo around the room as the camera zooms in on their faces. The tangerine sun gently sets and there is no doubt that they are perfect for one another. If only in real life it were as easy to know when you have found "the one"—just like in the movies. Unfortunately, there are no sure signs. As soon as you think you've found your soul mate, you immediately begin to wonder about the others still out there. Likewise, when you're single and out among the others, you're always looking for the "one."

Jason, 27, of Anaheim, California, remembers clearly when he met his wife, Jamie. "The first day I met Jamie, I went home and told my roommates I was going to marry this woman. I had never even thought about marriage in my whole life, but it was just one of those things. You may not believe it can happen, but it really did, and I knew I wanted to get to know her better. What's so strange is—being a pretty conservative guy—that was a very odd comment to come out of my mouth, but the connection I felt with Jamie was more than I had ever experienced before."

I asked Jason what advice he has for those seeking the right partner. "If you fast forwarded the relationship, it was very easy. That's the recommendation I give to people. Have a relationship that's easy. It's not going to be beautiful all the time, but it should be easy because you have common goals. The biggest difference I see between this relationship and any other relationship I've ever had is that it's easy and fun. It's like working with my best friend."

chantelle
armendanz, 18

favorite food:
mexican

biggest concern:
the leadership of
our country

favorite movie:
ladder 49

**best date
advice:** don't
move too fast,
be yourself, and
enjoy the night
to its fullest

**what you wish you
knew two years
ago:** absolutely
nothing. what
happened is over.
i would rather
know the future
instead.

life motto:
live life to its
fullest

Jason knew he had found the right partner when the relationship felt natural. It was not a fairytale, but, despite all of the bumps and hurdles, it moved along with ease. The key is to have a shared vision of what the relationship is and where it is going. This is a major point. I know many people who abandon relationships at the first sign of trouble. When a disagreement erupts, they walk. There's no willingness to work things out and grow from the experience. As a result, non-committed relationships dominate in our generation. We go from person to person enjoying the initial infatuation and "honeymoon" phase of the relationship, but back out and move on as soon as deeper issues of commitment and honesty arise.

While easy come, easy go relationships are not a beneficial lifelong strategy, according to John Gray, author of *Men are from Mars, Women are from Venus,* they do serve a purpose when you are in your early 20s. "The real key for people is not to place so much importance on these relationships as teenagers and in your early 20s. Ideally, wait till you are in the 24-27 range before you get serious about relationships," Gray told me during an interview.

"There is so much brain development that happens between 18-27. You really don't know what you want till you get up there in age. It's hard to know the right person, and it's hard for them to know if you are the right person. Unfortunately, even if you think you are lucky, you are still not ready to make a serious relationship work. The highest rate of divorce is people who get married in their early 20s. They don't know what they want yet.

"The 20s is a time to do what you want to do. If relationship is a part of that, then have relationships on your terms. Don't focus so much yet on making compromises and pleasing others. It should be more about learning how to be autonomous. Then when your brain develops around 27, you are really capable of knowing if this is the person for me."

As Gray points out, the first step you can take to find your ideal partner is to make an effort to know yourself. In fact, this is the answer to the majority of the quarterlife questions. How can you expect to recognize what you want in someone else if you don't even know what you want in yourself?

Looking back on my own relationships, it is clear that attraction was based on my own identity at the time. When I was trying to be Mr. GQ I dated Amy, a beauty queen who was a "good catch," because both of us were more interested in whom we were seen with than why we were together. Next came, Kathy, an adventurous girl who enjoyed rock climbing and mountain biking. She was a match because we both identified ourselves as outdoor adventurists. Then came Veronica, a "hippy girl" who talked poetry, politics, and music. She fed my interest in the arts and culture. Time and time again, as I reflect back, it's obvious that my personal identity was reflected in the partners and friends I embraced. Just like if you are at a big party with people of all nationalities. The tendency is to gravitate toward those who

john vogt, 27

favorite food: anything chocolate

biggest concern: my wife is pregnant and i worry about being a good father

what you wish you knew two years ago: it's okay not to have your mind made up

final thought: everyone can contribute to the beauty of life; just find your own way to do it

read more of what john had to share in "should i go for the big bucks or pursue want i truly want to do?"

speak English if that's your primary language. So too, in life, you will always gravitate towards those to whom you feel a connection. Jason instantly felt a rapport with Jamie, and that's why after the first meeting he told his friends he had met the woman he was going to marry.

The secret to being able to identify if your partner is the right one is to become clear on who you are. As Gray points out, casual dating in your early 20s can be a time to discover yourself. In addition, you may journal, meditate, take workshops, and go for walks to help "find yourself." Also read the chapter, "Who Am I?", to answer better this important question. Once you have peeled back the layers of who you are, it will be easier and clearer to know when your ideal partner enters into your life. As Brigitte Secard, 30, author of *Soulfire*, says so well, "We must find our own soul before we look for its soul mate."

Opportunity

Let's assume that you have taken steps to get to know your own likes, dislikes, values, strengths, and weaknesses. (If not, read the chapters "What is My Purpose?", "Does Becoming a Responsible Adult Mean Life Becomes Boring and Monotonous?" and "Who Am I?") To know if the person you are with is the right one, first ask yourself: *How do I feel when I am alone with myself?* Do you like your own company or does being alone make you antsy and uneasy? The bottom line is that you have to be comfortable with yourself before you can be comfortable with the companionship of someone else.

The second step is to ask *How do I feel when I am with him/her?* Is it an easy, fun, interesting, intimate, supportive, nurturing, and respectful relationship? Or is it hard, dull, boring, cold, competitive, painful, tiring, and trying? Often we base the compatibility of our relationships on the other person's profile: the job they have, books they've read, money they make, activities they pursue, places they travel, and so forth, and we forget to ask ourselves simply what it feels like when we are with him or her.

Next ask yourself: *Why are we together at this moment?* This is a big question that requires your complete honesty. Are you together because you are lonely or scared? Is it because you want someone to wash your clothes and take care of you? Do you need someone for your image? Perhaps you need someone to bring to dinner meetings, to please your parents, or to impress your friends?

Really—why are you together? Do you need each other to fill a void or do you genuinely want to be together? There is a big difference. In the latter case, you support each other in a similar vision. You desire to share your triumphs and tribulations with another. You both realize that being vulnerable and intimate is one of the most frightening yet rewarding of human experiences. An honest answer to *Why are we together at this moment?* will help you clearly see whether your partner is the right one.

Finally, I recommend you ask yourself: *What is my contribution to him/her in the relationship?* This question helps keep a balanced

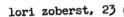

lori zoberst, 23

favorite food: macaroni and cheese

biggest concern: to be stuck in the same career path forever

what you wish you knew two years ago: the consequences of making hasty decisions

favorite movie: to many to list

best date advice: don't sweat the small things!

life motto: you're too important not to give yourself every possible chance!

perspective. It is very easy when trying to determine if another person is "right" for you to forget that a relationship also involves a sharing of yourself. If you discover that you are taking, taking, taking from the relationship without giving anything of yourself, then it is an unhealthy connection no matter how much you may enjoy it.

Likewise, you may discover that what you contribute to the relationship is not congruent with what you want your life to represent. For example, you may be demanding and controlling of your partner and for whatever reason he/she "gets off" on your insensitivity. No matter how much the relationship seems to work, if your top values are understanding and compassion, the relationship will inevitably distress you. You'll never be content as long as you continue living a contradiction between your values and actions.

Asking these four questions will help you become clearer if the person you're with is the right one.

CHAPTER EIGHTEEN

When should I marry?

"Life continues on earth, I think we've got some plans—but we will see," were the only words that soft spoken cosmonaut Yuri Malenchenko muttered when asked about his marriage. Yuri had just returned from a six-month space trip in which he and his fiancé were married by a satellite video link from space. Now with his feet firmly planted back on Earth, Yuri and his wife are beginning a new phase of their lives—as a married couple.

Whether it's a satellite video link to space, a Las Vegas drive-thru window, a private church in Italy, or the back of a motorcycle, there are endless ways that people are getting married today. In fact, I read about a couple who married while skydiving! (Imagine their wedding night.) But regardless of how many ways there are to get married one question still begs to be answered—*When should I marry?*

Nathan, 26, and Madeline, 23, had been married for one week when I met them. "I knew I had found my best friend, someone I wanted to see the world with, so I asked him to marry me," Madeline told me. Likewise Nathan added, "For me it was right because I fell in love with this girl. We have such an unbelievable connection. I love her so much and I just knew it was the right time."

Both Nathan and Madeline spoke of love as being the reason they married, but how do you define love? We hear the word all the time. Before Brad Nowell of *Sublime* died from an overdose his song about love, "What I Got?", topped the charts. Robbie Williams did the same with his song "Real Love." So did the Beatles, Beyonce, Black

ganae vigil, 19

favorite food: mashed potatoes

biggest concern: what the world will be like when i'm old

best date advice: keep them guessing

worst date advice: putting everything out in the open... moving too fast

what you wish you knew two years ago: not to try to grow up too soon

life motto: life is a dance you learn as you go

Eyed Peas, Bob Marley, and Boyz II Men. All of these artists sang about love, but what is it?

Is love the feeling you get when you see a hot girl dancing at a club or a tan stud working outside? Is your love for ice cream the same as love in marriage? Is it love when you hi-five after a touchdown or hug after a softball win? Is love a feeling that comes and goes based on physical attraction? Is love even real?

I asked Marianne Williamson, *New York Times* #1 best selling author of *Return to Love*, how she defined love. "I would never seek to define love, but I know it when I feel it," she told me. "When I judge another person, that is not love; when I try controlling another person, that is not love; when I fail to honor, bless, and care for another person; that is not love. When I see those energies in myself and say, 'Get off it. Let that go,' then something happens in my environment. The words I could use to describe it are words like peace, harmony, comfort, growth, nurturing, and nourishment. None of those things define love, but I think they all characterize love."

Williamson hits on a key point. Love is not about manipulating or playing games with another person. It's not about getting something from someone. It's not even about someone making us feel complete. It's about giving of your attention, patience, support, and time.

Too often we define love by how another person makes us feel. If they are good to us and make us feel orgasmic we feel like we're in love. But the moment they let us down or when the "magic" wears off, we move on thinking the love is gone. The truth is the only way we can experience true love with another person is if we give love.

John Lennon and Paul McCartney wrote in a song, "The love you take is equal to the love you make." I agree. When I was 21 and working as a camp counselor near Santa Cruz, California, I experienced the truth of this statement. The other counselors and I used to do a campfire activity where I would take a large sheet of colored paper and cut a heart out of it. The heart signified love. Then I would tear the paper heart in two pieces and give one piece to another person and keep one piece. Next, both I and the person I gave the piece to would tear our pieces in half giving away one and keeping the other. This continued on as, tear by tear, the single heart began to spread to all 150 kids and counselors around the campfire. Soon everyone had a piece of paper (love) and as they tore it in half and gave it away suddenly each person would receive 5 pieces then 10, 30, and 40 pieces at a time. It was impossible to give away the heart because the more that was given the more that returned.

The same thing happens when you give love in life. **You give love when you put the interests and concerns of another person above your own. When you are able to do this, you are ready for marriage.** The question isn't *Will this person make me happy?* but instead *Am I ready to be this person's lover?* Am I ready to support this person for a lifetime? Am I ready to raise children with this person for a

**august cheeser,
20**

hometown:
tuscon, az

favorite food:
salmon fillet

biggest concern:
future state of
america given the
current trends

favorite movie:
waking life

**worst date
advice:** order
dishes with
spinach

favorite band:
terry taylor

life motto: just
relax

lifetime? Am I ready to listen to and respect this person for a lifetime? Am I ready to empathize with and work to understand this person for a lifetime?

When you and your partner both answer yes to the above questions you are already married. It doesn't take a ceremony, guest list, reception, and document to get married. All those do is provide tax breaks and signify to the world that you and your partner have made a commitment to one another. True marriage has everything to do with the commitment you personally make to your partner and little to do with the color of napkins at your reception.

Opportunity

Every week there's a star's wedding featured on the cover of a grocery store aisle magazine. Whether it's Jennifer Lopez, Britney Spears, or simply a friend of yours, people often tell us they were ready for marriage when they found that special someone who made them feel complete. Unfortunately, according to the experts I've spoken with, neither love nor marriage works that way. Instead of expecting another person to round out your rough edges, true marriage occurs when you put the needs and interests of your partner equal to your own.

How do you put another's interests equal to your own? How do you prepare yourself for true marriage? Chuck Sorenson, a minister and psychologist, taught me to begin asking the question: *How is he/she giving or calling for love right now?* with each interaction I have, especially with a significant other. For example, the next time you are in disagreement with your partner ask the question: *How is her yelling at me a giving or calling for love?* You may realize that it's a calling for love. Perhaps you've been busy with work and haven't spent much time with her. The only way she's been able to get through to you in the past is by yelling. Now the same pattern is occurring. Her verbal outburst is a call for love and attention. Or, on the other hand, suppose he scolds you for not wearing a helmet when riding your mountain bike. By asking *How is he giving or calling for love when he scolds me?* you'll discover that it's really because he cares and is concerned about your safety. It's his way of giving love.

When you see another's actions in the context of love, you'll judge less harshly and be better able to receive them into your life. It sounds simple, but—trust me—it is profound. Everything we do is a giving or calling for love. When you recognize this in your partner, you're ready for marriage.

AGE 33

HOMETOWN Waseca, MN

FAVORITE FOOD Cheese & CAFÉ BREVÉS!

LAST READ Autobiography Of A Fat Bride :
OF A ~~PRETEND~~ PRETEND ADULTHOOD. by Laurie
Lance Armstrong's Its not about the bike.

BIGGEST CONCERN
As long as I have my health, I have
~~everything I just enjoy~~ working as a nur
many people with irreversible health problem
everyday I'm able to count my blessings. my bigge
lose my health.

FAVORITE MOVIE Amelie, Napoleon Dynamite, Wh
Happy Gilmore, foreign flics, funny flics, the
many to list!

BEST DATE ADVICE
Hmm.... I've pretty much been in comitted
most of my adult life and haven't "dated"
let you know the "best date advice" when I f

WORST DATE ADVICE
Again, Dont know. The only advice I can gi
would be to love people deeply & have no
you've loved well and with all your heart.

DIFFERENCE BETWEEN OUR GENERATION AND OUR PARENTS li u
music, tattoos & starbucks

technology;
of course

WHAT YOU WISH YOU WOULD HAVE KNOWN TWO YEARS AGO

That life is a wave - sometimes taking
shores you'd have never guessed - go with
trust it.

LIFE MOTTO

"Go confidently in the direction of yo
dreams"

CHAPTER NINETEEN

What is the key to a successful marriage?

A local church sponsored an evening question-and-answer session on marriage last February. Couples who had been together for 40, 50, and even 60 years were at the front of the room fielding questions from the audience of newlyweds and young couples. When asked by a 24-year-old, "What is the key to a successful marriage?" an older gentleman smiled and simply replied, "You have to realize that you're going to have good *decades* and bad *decades!*"

While the gentleman was making a joke, a half century of marriage is not. It's hard to imagine being together with someone for nearly twice as long as most of us have been alive. When you are 25, a two-year relationship seems like a long time, just as waiting a month for your birthday seemed like an eternity when you were six.

I asked Zig Ziglar, considered one of the greatest speakers and success coaches of the 20th Century, and author of *See You at the Top,* for the secret to his 56-year marriage. "Start by understanding that men and women are dramatically different," Ziglar said to me. "Despite the fact that we say that, we often treat each other alike. For example, I say to the ladies, 'When your husband has been knocked flat on his back, when he's lower than a snake's belly, when his self-image is down to zero, if at that specific time you will become the aggressor, come onto him strong and make it crystal clear that despite the fact that he suffered a little setback you still find him irresistibly attractive, there is nothing that will

nneka okonkwo, 23

hometown:
portland, or

favorite food:
chocolate

biggest concern:
not having
financial
security or a
career that is
rewarding

best date advice:
know how to have
a good time by
yourself.

**what you wish you
knew two years
ago:** that it's
okay to mess up
and change your
mind

life motto:
success is a
journey

build a man's ego and confidence like that will.' But fellows need to know that if you take the same approach when your wife has been knocked flat on her back, when she is really in the dumps, if you come onto her strong, it will set your marriage back at least five, maybe ten, years. Because what she's thinking is, 'Here I am. I've got all these troubles and all he thinks about is himself.' Men and women are different and we need to understand this."

While Ziglar's and the church couples' marriages have lasted decade after decade, the sad fact of the matter is that 50-year anniversaries are becoming a rarity. The highest rate of divorce exists in the quarterlife generation, those of us who married in our late teens and early 20s. So while reaching your golden anniversary may be a distant half-century away, you can certainly learn from other successful marriages.

Mindy and Don married the month after our high school graduation. I remember going to their wedding thinking *How can they possibly be ready for marriage? I barely know how to tie my shoelaces and they are tying the knot.* The following year, at age 19, Mindy was pregnant with their first child, Rachel, and over the next eight years she gave birth to two more children. Now ten years later, despite the trend of our generation she is still happily married. I asked Mindy why her marriage has been so successful.

"It's got to be our communication and respect. Communication is something you definitely have to keep working at. Listening is the biggest part, but we also respect each other's feelings and ideas. Maybe we don't always agree, but I respect what he has to say and visa versa. I think that whether it's a friendship or the relationship you have with your spouse, that's a big thing."

Respect in a relationship begins with respect for yourself. As Nido Qubein, author of *How to be a Great Communicator* and chairman of Great Harvest Bread Company, says, "In order to sell yourself to anyone, first you have to sell

yourself to yourself." When you realize that your life matters and that you are here for a purpose, the way you walk and talk changes. You begin to live by the Golden Rule, "Do unto others as you would have them do unto you." This comes automatically because you treat others with the same respect that you treat yourself. In fact, you expect others to do the same and won't tolerate anyone who treats you otherwise.

This is a key point. **If you come into a relationship healthy and balanced, you are more likely to attract a partner who together with you can make a successful relationship possible.**

Here's a little test. Next time you are in a restaurant, look around and watch couples. Notice the couples sitting silently, staring off at the wall over their partners' shoulders, as if they have been given a life sentence without parole. Look at their eyes and body language. Do they seem alive or aloof?

Then, locate the couples where one partner is obviously dominating

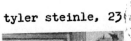

tyler steinle, 23

hometown:
sturgis, sd

favorite song:
otherside by the
red hot chili
peppers

biggest concern:
making myself and
others happy

favorite book:
frankenstein

**difference
between our
generation and
our parents:** i
think we have
more things
available to us,
but the decisions
we have to make
are harder.

life motto: live
life one day at a
time

and controlling the conversation. What does the other person seem to be thinking? Is their demeanor saying, "I really support you," or, "I wish you would shut up for once."

Finally, look around the room and notice the couples engaging one another back and forth. Now, chances are that this latter group falls into one of two categories. The first category is new relationships where the infatuation and "best behavior" still exists. The second category is couples that share a mutual passion and interest for their lives as well as their partners' lives. Those in the second category are some of the most content people I have met in my life.

What could form a better foundation for a long, supportive, and passionate marriage than supporting, learning, sharing, and growing with another person?

Opportunity

When you treat yourself and your partner with respect, your entire interaction and way of being together is transformed.

Paul Argentiere, author of *The Get It Together Process*, taught me the following exercise for fostering respect and communication in your relationship.

Begin by sitting across from one another at a table and placing three pieces of paper in front of you. Write your partner's name on one piece of paper, your name on the next, and both of your names on the third. Take out the paper with your partner's name on it and look him or her in the eye and ask *What empowers you?* For the next five minutes, while writing down the responses on the sheet of paper, listen and prompt the question over and over again. If your partner has trouble starting, resist your urge to give suggestions. Instead, just listen and smile.

There should be no limitation to the responses. If you are a mother of two, but have always thought it would be empowering to bicycle across the United States, then by all means say so when it's your turn!

Once your partner has finished listing all of the activities, places,

people, and beliefs that he or she finds empowering, pass over the pen. Now it's your turn. Taking out the sheet with your name on it have your partner ask and write your responses to the question: *What empowers you?*

The power of doing this exercise is that it brings to the surface the dreams and ambitions you both have. Two things will happen immediately. First, it rekindles an interest and spark inside of you to *carpe diem* or seize the day. Second, it allows your partner to see you in a whole new light. Undoubtedly, your partner will learn about aspirations he or she never knew you had and vice versa. Few things foster respect better than honoring and understanding the depth of interests and determination in another person.

The final part of the exercise is to take out the third piece of paper with both names on it and together write down ways that you can support each other's empowerment lists. Remember how you want to be supported may be different from what your partner wants.

jo leigh ureel, 21

hometown:
detroit, mi

**favorite
food:** cheese,
chocolate, and
ranch dressing,
but not always
together

biggest concern:
politics in the
united states

**best date
advice:** wear your
favorite shoes

**worst date
advice:**
dating your
best friend's
boyfriend's
friend

secret to life:
smile

As Ziglar pointed out men and women are different. This is not an eye-for-an-eye and a tooth-for-a-tooth exchange where you must do one action in return for an equal action from you partner. Instead, consider the ways that you want to help and support your partner, simply because you have a renewed respect and interest in him or her. By creating this third list, you will automatically notice your perceptions towards one another gravitate deeper into respect and gratitude.

CHAPTER TWENTY]

When is it time to end a relationship?

Do you remember the Lorena and John Wayne Bobbit case? Jealous over John's affair, Lorena cut off his penis while he slept, and then drove away, tossing the penis out her car window. Surely this was a strong sign there were serious issues to work out in the relationship! It makes you wonder, "Why were they still together?"

Lorena and John are not alone. The same thing recently happened in Manila, Philippines, when Antonio Uanesiras, age 30, woke up to find his penis cut off after his wife found another woman's text message on his mobile phone. Obviously, having a body part lopped off by your partner is good indication you should end a relationship, but how do you know when it's time to end a relationship that is less dramatic?

"You hit a point when you know it's time," Collin, age 28, explained to me. "I can't explain it, other than to tell you I just knew. I still love her. I care about her, and I want her to be happy, but I am not in love with her. It got to the point where I didn't want to be around her anymore. I would do anything to avoid coming home, because I didn't want to see her and she didn't want to see me."

Collin and Rachel had been married for five years. High school sweethearts, they went separate ways after graduation only to find their paths reuniting. Shortly after they married, their first son was born, and he was followed a few years later by a second son. For Collin ending the relationship was

jason regier, 29

biggest concern: following my passion and making a living at it

what you'll be doing in five years: married, running my own business, getting paid to do what i love, and on my way to financial independence.

life motto: do what you can, where you are, with what you have

read more of what jason had to share in "how can i make my 'mark' in this world?"

difficult, but because the family was severed, it became even harder.

"Going forward with the separation was one of the hardest things I have ever done," said Collin. "You get comfortable with the way things are, even if they are not making both of you happy. When we were going forward with the divorce I talked to a guy at the bar who told me, 'Collin, whatever you do, don't back down. Do it.' The guy had been married for over 20 years and was now going through a divorce that he had wanted 15 years earlier. On several occasions, he had started to end the relationship, but he backed down each time. Now he's realized that he and his wife have been miserable because neither had the guts to end it."

We all can relate to the man at the bar. How many people do you know who are in a relationship simply because the security of being "with" someone outweighs the pain of the relationship? Many of us would rather be with a partner and miserable than to be alone. It's sad, but true. Ending a relationship isn't just about the connection between two people. It also carries a lot of baggage, such as a feeling of having failed and fears that you may never find someone "better" and will live the rest of your life as an "old maid" or a "hermit."

"When we ended our relationship, I couldn't stop crying," Amanda, 27, a reporter, who just ended a six-month relationship, told me. "It was like someone ripped my chest open and poured salt in. It hurt like hell. I knew it was the best decision for both of us, but yeah, part of me had regrets. Maybe it would have worked if I had taken more time off from work, if I had paid more attention to him, if I had … but I know that I really tried and he tried, too. It just wasn't going to work for us right now. We are different people who want different things."

I asked Amanda if she felt like a failure. "Do I feel like I've failed? Yeah, parts of me do, but I know in a couple of months I'll look back with few regrets because both of us did try to make it work. It's not like it caught either of us off guard. As difficult as it is to leave now, we

both realize that we'd be happier in the long run with someone else."

Ending a relationship is never easy. It rocks your core. But I have discovered that people, like Amanda, are able to do it with some peace of mind because they honestly tried to develop the relationship. They were willing to roll up their sleeves and work on their issues together.

On the other side of the coin, there are many couples that call it quits at the first sign of difficulty. Never allowing a relationship to grow and establish a solid foundation, they run from infatuation to infatuation. Too often, they marry only to divorce a year or two later. The problem is that relationships aren't always going to be like a Disney movie. There are going to be high times and low times. Often, it's while going through the low times that the love couples experience for one another really blossoms.

I am continuously amazed at the number of people I meet in their 20s who have been divorced once and even twice. When I ask them why, I hear comments like,

crystal smith, 17

favorite food: chocolate chip cookie dough ice cream

biggest concern: what college to go to and what grade to teach

favorite book: a wrinkle in time

impact you want to have: to change people's lives for the better

difference between our generation and our parents: we have more conveniences and are lazier

life motto: to have no regrets

"I didn't like feeling tied down anymore," "She lost her job and things became tight," "All he wants to do is sit around watching the television," "I met someone who makes me feel stronger (or sexier)." All of these could be valid reasons to end a relationship, or they could be excuses to avoid digging in and working out issues. There appears to be a razor's edge to walk between knowing when to end a relationship and when to invest in its future.

I asked Marilyn Innerfeld, a mother and author of *Healing Through Love*, about this razor's edge. Having been married for over 30 years, I was curious how she and her husband recently decided to end the relationship. "I did work very hard on our relationship," Innerfeld told me. "We were married for 31 years before it ended. The bottom line came back to the simple question 'Does this bring me joy?' We were coming into such powerful disagreements time and again that the joys were so much smaller." She continued, "There was no joy left. It was a mutual separation. We could have been like the average couple and stayed married for the next 30 years and, from the outside looking in, nobody would have known, but it wasn't fun anymore. There was nothing to come home to that made my heart sing."

It is time to end a relationship when the opportunities to deepen your connection and growth give way to feelings of emptiness. Being together should not be like entering a black hole that drains your life and energy. Amanda knew the relationship was over when she acknowledged that her goals were different from her partner. Both Collin and Innerfeld knew their relationships were over when the thought of going home to their partners contained no juice. Each marriage had become void of any anticipation or passion.

Opportunity

The following three steps will help you navigate the fine line between ending a relationship and continuing forward with it.

The first step is to ask Innerfeld's simple and powerful question: *Does*

this bring me joy? Joy does not mean that you have to be happy all the time. Rather, the question means: Does it fulfill, nurture, expand, support, and encourage me? Also flip the question around and ask yourself: *Am I fulfilling, nurturing, expanding, supporting, and encouraging my partner?* Remember relationships are as much about giving as receiving.

Now, before you get on the phone and break up with your partner, take a moment and look closer. A relationship with these characteristics can still be challenging and difficult on occasion. The key is that both of you are becoming more whole and content as a couple and as individuals through the low periods.

The second step is to ask *Am I experiencing joy, or not experiencing joy, because of the relationship or because of my life right now?* This is important. Your emptiness and lack of anticipation may have little to do with your partner and everything to do with the fact that you have been burning the candle at both ends; lost your job; achieved a lifelong goal,

logan lamphere, 27

favorite book: farmer's boy by laura ingalls wilder

biggest concern: deteriorating families

what you wish you knew two years ago: not to worry as much—everything will be fine

life motto: you won't know if you will like it, if you don't try first

read more of what logan had to share in "should i travel and explore before settling down?"

only to find it shallow; been eating poorly; stopped working out; not seen the sunlight for several weeks; and so forth. If you haven't been taking care of yourself, not only is it unfair, it is also foolish, to expect a relationship to bring you joy.

The final step is to ask two questions: *Why should we stay together?* and *Why should we end the relationship?* As you write out the answers, the best decision will become obvious to you. The key to clearly seeing the answer is to be brutally honest with yourself in steps one and two.

After you've completed all three steps, I recommend sleeping on your decision a night or two and looking at your lists again before taking action. (In the middle of an emotional situation your judgment can be distorted.) If the same decision surfaces over and over, chances are good that you should listen to it.

CHAPTER TWENTY-ONE

When should I have children?

"First comes love, then comes marriage, then comes Tammy in a baby carriage." Sadly, not everyone who has children is ready for them. Recently, a Taiwanese man was suspended from eBay when he tried to auction off three Vietnamese girls. He placed the starting bid at $5,400 and posted it for several days before it was discovered and shut down.

It's obvious that some people should be banned from having children, but what about the rest of us? As quarterlifers we have rewritten the rules of parenthood. Only a generation ago, it was not uncommon for our parents and grandparents to have one or more children by the time they were 20 years old. Now, however, more and more quarterlifers are planning to wait until their 30s, or even early 40s, before having children.

One of the reasons for this delay is emotional maturity, as Ethan Watters, author of *Urban Tribes,* points out. "Maturity is a more valuable parenting asset than physical stamina. Yes, parenting is a physical challenge, but it is first and foremost an emotional challenge. Having the energy to weather the many crises of raising children is less important than having the poise to stay calm throughout."

In my opinion, raising children is one of the noblest pursuits, and also one of the most challenging. Children by their nature are selfish. They live in their own worlds and expect their own needs to be taken care of above all else. What makes this so difficult for a parent who is a quarterlifer is that you are just venturing into the real world and trying to take care of your own needs. Think about it. In the midst

vivian jolley, 22

current home:
miami, fl

biggest concern:
the future of
healthcare in
america and the
loss of family
values

best date advice:
always stay true
to yourself. you
should always
be learning
from each other.
actions always
speak louder than
words

life motto: the
day you cease to
speak is the day
you begin to die.

read more of what
vivian had to
share in "how can
i make my 'mark'
in this world?"

of figuring out "Who am I?" "What is my purpose?" "What is the meaning of life?" you are also caring for another human being whose very survival depends on you. Often this is overwhelming for young parents, and so it becomes a case of the blind leading the blind.

This was the situation for Albert Galvan, 20, who grew up in a neglectful and abusive home. At six years of age he became the man of the house when his young mother separated from his alcoholic father. From that point forward, Albert frequently supported his emotionally unstable mother until, at age 17, his 14-year-old girlfriend Cassandra—also from a dysfunctional home of young parents—became pregnant. The two of them lived in a rundown garage apartment until Cassandra gave birth to a healthy baby girl.

The hospital, however, was the first and last place that Albert spent any length of time with his newborn daughter. The following day the state took Albert and Cassandra's baby and placed her in a foster home.

The only hope Albert and Cassandra had of seeing their daughter again was to prove to the state that they were responsible and worthy parents. But two years later, after a string of missed parenting classes, failed drug tests, and a lack of displayed responsibility, the state ruled to terminate their rights to raising the baby girl. Is it any wonder? Neither Albert or Cassandra had any stability in their lives growing up. Both came from the homes of young parents who were not emotionally ready to raise children.

On the flip side of this issue, many quarterlifers *are* ready for children. In my interviews, several 20- and 30-year-olds expressed how they attained a sense of completeness when they had children. "I can't explain it, but I know it's what I am here to do," one mother told me. "For the first time, I feel like my life has meaning," said a father.

So, how will you know when you should have a child? **It seems, as Watters pointed out, that the best determining factor for having children is whether** **you're emotionally ready.** More than money, the quality of your neighborhood, or how old you are, the most important question is: "Are you ready to devote yourself to raising a child?"

"I don't think that it's necessarily about having everything in place," Travis, a 27-year-old high school science teacher, told me. "I've heard from so many people, 'Don't wait until you're financially ready, because you never will be.' So, I don't know if it's so much about our waiting for things to be in place as much as our waiting until we are ready for it. Being a schoolteacher, I see too many kids who have parents who shouldn't be parents because they don't put the time into it and their kids don't come first."

He continued, "I've got the feeling that whenever I have kids it'll be when I am willing to sacrifice my time for my kids for the next 20 years. It's funny how it becomes more appealing. If you had asked me a year or two ago, I would have said that I had no desire to have kids. That's changed and I don't know if it's because friends around

kevin wilmot, 29

hometown:
kalispell, mt

favorite food:
lobster

biggest concern:
providing for
my wife and
daughter. i want
to make sure my
daughter has a
good life.

last read:
plato's republic

**lesson you
learned as a
college wrestling
all-american:**
hard work pays
off

life motto:
learn from your
mistakes

me started having kids or just getting older, but kids look cuter. It became a little more appealing."

Travis and his wife are among those who won't be caught off guard. Like other quarterlifers, they have taken the time to reflect together on the pros and cons of having children. For some quarterlifers, this reflection encourages them to begin a family. They recognize that nothing would give them more satisfaction than bringing another life into the world. For others, the reflection process leads to waiting, because they have goals and dreams they are devoted to completing first. This waiting is the reason why our generation has delayed having children nearly twice as long as previous generations. It is neither right nor wrong. Rather it is just a choice we are making.

Opportunity

Television ads claim that the Peace Corps is "the hardest job you'll ever love." Perhaps this also applies to raising children. There are four qualities I have witnessed in outstanding parents. They are patience, consistency, love, and respect. These qualities correlate with what psychologist and author Daniel Goleman calls Emotional Intelligence, which includes self-awareness, impulse control, persistence, self-motivation, empathy, and social deftness. According to Goleman, "These are the qualities that mark people who excel in real life."

The following list of questions will help you decide if you and your partner are emotionally ready for children.

T or F
Under pressure I stay relaxed and composed.

T or F
I am willing to compromise my dreams to raise and care for children.

T or F
I can see my partner and myself working as a team in raising children.

T or F
I am able to see a situation from other people's viewpoint especially my partner's and be sensitive to it.

T or F
I respect my partner's opinions and actions.

T or F
I believe I would be a positive influence in the life of my children.

T or F
I calm myself quickly when angered.

T or F
I communicate my needs and feelings honestly.

T or F
My partner and I have discussed in depth our views and values on having and raising children.

T or F
I am aware of how my behavior impacts other people.

If the majority of your answers (seven or greater) were true, you have a high degree of emotional intelligence and are better suited for raising children. If you answered false to the majority of questions, I encourage you to pick up Daniel's book, *Emotional Intelligence*, to learn how to develop further your emotional maturity.

In the end, there are few pursuits as honorable as raising children. The challenge is deciding if and when you are ready, and the solution lies in recognizing when you are emotionally ready, willing, and interested in bringing children into this world.

paula langlois, 21

hometown:
rhinelander, wi

favorite movie:
13 going on 30

biggest concern:
finishing school strong

favorite food:
mashed potatoes

what you wish you knew two years ago: you have to pay back your credit cards

life motto: you haven't lived until you've totaled three cars

CHAPTER TWENTY-TWO

What should I do for a living?

"It's all just a big misunderstanding. I wasn't trying to pass off the bill. That's ridiculous," Alice Pike told the police as they hauled her off to jail. Alice was arrested at a Wal Mart after trying to purchase $1,675 worth of items with a fake 1 million dollar bill. The clerk reported that she even wanted the change back! When asked from jail why she tried using the novelty bill, Alice replied, "You just can't keep up with the US Treasury."

Wouldn't it be great if money were easy to acquire, if we could get something for nothing, and if a 50¢ novelty bill at the grocery store was really worth $1 million? Unfortunately, that's not the case. To earn money, most of us have to work. That's a fact of life. What isn't a fact of life is whether or not we will enjoy the work we choose.

You will spend a major part of your life working. Think about it: 40 hours a week, month after month, and year after year. This is why it's so important to find a fulfilling vocation and not just *another* job.

"When I was a kid I remember my dad telling me. 'Do something you like because you're going to be working more than you're not working,'" Charlie Daniels of the *Charlie Daniels Band* told me. Daniels knows what he is talking about. Since he started playing in a band back in 1959, he has topped both the rock and country music charts, toured the country, and written three books. Now, 68-years-old, he is still going strong. Last year he played over 160 gigs. That's nearly one show every other day of the year!

nathan steinle, 25

biggest concern: finding a good education program

what you wish you knew two years ago: enjoy each and every day because the hard times are sometimes the best times

worst date advice: cheesy lines like, "did it hurt. . . when you fell from heaven?"

life motto: keep on charging the enemy so long as there is life!

read more of what nathan had to share in "what is my spiritual path?"

Daniels discovered a career he enjoys, but is he the exception to the rule? Is it possible for the rest of us to find the perfect job, too?

"People think that there's one right job out there for them. What I've experienced and helped others to see is that we have core strengths, core talents, and passions inside of us, but there is no perfect career," job consultant Cynthia Ryk explained to me. "We live in a world where we have lots of choices, which means we have a variety of ways in which we can express those talents."

As Ryk points out, it's not about finding "the one" perfect job, instead it's about moving in the direction of your interests and talents. Perhaps you can find a number of different jobs that will be equally fulfilling. The bottom line is that three hurdles keep you from discovering what you should do for a living.

The first hurdle is identifying your core strengths, talents, and passions. For help, I recommend reviewing the chapters: "Who Am I?", "What Is My Purpose?", and "Does Being a Responsible Adult Mean Life Becomes Boring and Monotonous?" The second hurdle arises when you are locked into the belief that there is only one job out there that will make you happy. Thus, you miss new career possibilities that present themselves. The third hurdle is that you're simply afraid of pursing your dream career.

"I truly believe that everyone has a purpose and passion that lies within them, but there is a lot of fear around pursuing it," Megan, a 28-year-old who left her successful massage therapy practice to pursue a degree in somatic psychology told me. "There is the risk of the world saying 'tough shit' to our dreams. It's hard to continue when the world doesn't seem very supportive, but I think that's part of the process: being able to put it out there, and pursue what feels right, even though the world may not accept it."

Megan voiced what few of us want to admit. The greatest obstacle in finding a perfect career is our fear of pursuing it. "What if I fail?" "What if they are right?" "What if I can't support my family?" "What

if I discover it's not right for me after all?" These kinds of "what if" questions paralyze us. If we give in to them, they prevent us from pursuing our career dreams and we end up taking the secure road, the road of least risk.

As quarterlifers, we are a generation that has witnessed many of our parents fall prey to this fear. We have seen them ignore their passions and chase the golden carrot of job security. We have seen them commit to 30 years of misery, only to get laid off a year before receiving their retirement packages. Having witnessed this, we've promised ourselves not to follow in their footsteps. "Quality of life," "job satisfaction," "fulfillment," and "meaning" have become our mantras. Our generation wants change, and we won't tolerate lip service without action behind it.

For quarterlifers, the key to experiencing a high quality of life is to take baby steps and recognize that finding our career is a journey. We don't have to get it right the first time. Rather, each step we take exposes the next step.

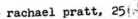

rachael pratt, 25

favorite movie:
goonies

biggest concern:
raising my
daughter to be
feeling when the
world is numb

**worst date
advice:** order a
salad and laugh
at all his jokes

favorite book:
the amazing
adventures of
kavalier and clay
by michael chabon

life motto:
don't lie, don't
gossip, don't
cheat, live,
love, laugh,
dance as if today
is your last

Like Indiana Jones in *Indiana Jones and the Last Crusade,* on occasion the next step may be a leap of faith, but we can trust that the bridge will appear.

Charlie Daniels knows this is true. When he first tried breaking into the music business he was one of thousands of other hopefuls. Daniels knew he had to take a leap of faith, as he explains, "I think a lot of the time people are afraid to cut the apron strings and make a commitment. That's what it takes. It takes a commitment: 'I'm going to do this. I believe in what I'm doing and who I am.' You've got to start there. If you don't make a commitment, it just isn't going to happen for you."

Daniels' first leap was moving to Nashville to play backup guitar in a recording studio. After making this commitment, he soon found himself backing up Bob Dylan. Realizing this was the opportunity of a lifetime, Daniels seized it. "You've got to take advantage of a situation," he told me. "That's what happened with me. I was hungry. I was the guy that most wanted to be where I was at that time. Everybody was honored to be playing with Bob Dylan, but to a lot of the guys it was just another session. To me that was *the day,* and I was cognizant of it."

Bob Dylan was so impressed with Daniels' guitar playing that he asked him to stay and record the rest of the album with him. This boost of confidence was one of the most significant events that propelled Daniels forward into pursuing his successful career.

Every job you have matters! It's as simple as that. Daniels, Ryk, and Megan all know this. Unfortunately, many in our generation don't seem to believe it. During street interviews for my television program, I commonly hear quarterlifers say, "It's just a starter job. My first job doesn't really matter." They believe that it's not until we reach our late 30s, 40s, and 50s that what we're doing really counts. The danger in this belief is that we miss out on opportunities as they arise.

If Daniels had just been "serving time" at the recording studio, he would not have taken advantage of Dylan's visit. Likewise, if you view your perfect career as something that will occur in 20 years, you will miss out on today's opportunities. Instead, see your career as a process. Take advantage of today's opportunities while moving forward towards tomorrow.

Let's face it. The world is forgiving of youth. As quarterlifers, we can stumble, start over, and change our minds much easier than a 60-year-old man or woman. So there is no better time in our lives to take a leap of faith towards our dream careers.

Opportunity

The Grand Canyon didn't develop as the result of a single event, and neither will your perfect job. They both are processes. The Grand Canyon has formed through years of continuous erosion. Likewise, discovering what you should do for a living is an ongoing journey of introspection followed by trial and error.

One secret on the journey is: Go for it! Once you've identified your interests and talents, then begin

brahim marsh, 26

home country:
morocco

favorite food:
italian

biggest concern:
getting my
business started

best date advice:
take her to a
nice movie and
dinner

**what you wish you
knew two years
ago:** life is too
short

life motto:
family

seeking jobs, businesses, and/or volunteer positions that match your skills. Instead of succumbing to paralysis by analysis, get involved. Nothing will give you immediate feedback like actually performing the positions in which you are interested.

There are two things you should be aware of as you try new positions. First, be honest with yourself. Don't confuse the initial excitement of a new experience with the satisfaction of doing a job that truly fulfills you. It is best to stay with a job for at least a month or two to get an accurate feel for it.

The second step is to keep your eyes and ears open. When you take action towards a position, unseen opportunities will suddenly arise. It works like magic! As the old saying goes, "When God closes one door, He always opens a window." Be on the lookout for fresh ways to express your talents and interests. A great question to ask each night is *What did I do today that I really enjoyed and how can I make a living doing more of it in the future?*

CHAPTER TWENTY-THREE]

Can I be in a relationship and still be successful?

"I avoided one car after another by flashing my lights at them," said 29-year-old Heath Dequied. "It was impossible to slow down! Stomping on the brakes proved pointless, nothing worked."

Heath raced across 125 miles of crowded highway when his cruise control stuck and kept his car traveling at speeds over 120 miles per hour. Fortunately, after frantically swerving in and out of traffic for over an hour, the car finally shut down and Heath was able to safely pull off the highway.

Have you ever felt like Heath? As if you're trapped speeding down the superhighway of life? Maybe you're on the fast track to graduation and have stopped dating to prevent yourself from getting sidetracked. Or perhaps you just graduated and

are quickly making your way up the corporate ladder. You'd like to have a family but are afraid of losing your momentum and focus at work. Underlying both of these situations is the question, "Is it possible to pursue my personal interests and be in a relationship at the same time?"

Dani, 21, a senior at Southern Oregon University in Ashland, Oregon, has felt the pressure of this question. As a media major, she's been trying to find a balance between her school work and dating life over the past year. "I think it's easier to do what you want to do when single," she told me. "When in a relationship it's easy to settle for something less instead of doing what you want to do in life. But it also depends on how dedicated you and your partner are. Last year I was

kate fejfar, 23

hometown:
crestwood, ky

favorite food:
ice cream

biggest concern:
am i fulfilling
my purpose in
life as i should/
could be?

**worst date
advice:** date
someone only on
attraction

favorite book:
charlotte's web

**what you wish you
knew two years
ago:** what an
awesome place i'd
be in now

life motto:
you can't do
it on your own
strength!

in a serious relationship and I did well in school at the same time. I gave up hanging out with friends and stopped doing extra things like dance and art class. It's about finding balance and ultimately it's a compromise."

Dani voiced what many quarterlifers fear. We've come to believe that being in a relationship means giving up parts of our lives. Whether it means backing off from studies, work, friends, or hobbies, we fear that by entering into a relationship we have to sacrifice aspects of our life. I asked Kathlyn Hendricks, a busy woman who travels the country giving seminars and has co-authored with her husband over ten books including the book *Lasting Love*, if she believes it's possible to be in a relationship and still excel as an individual. "That is one of the big issues for most people," she told me. "'What happens to me as an individual when I get in a relationship? Do I disappear in the relationship and get swallowed up by the other person?' In our work and our own relationship we teach people how to do the relationship dance and really experience a sense of union with another person and also to be separate and have your own individual experience in the world."

Hendricks went on to tell me, "The great gift of a close relationship is that it opens up the opportunity to be truly creative. In most relationships, energy is wasted in a power struggle of blaming: who's right and who's wrong. That eats up a tremendous amount of creative energy. But if you join together and move into the world together it liberates creative energy that you can use for your own projects and supporting your partner. There is an infinite amount of creative energy. It's not limited."

Following Hendricks' comments I asked her husband, Gay, "Why is it, if you look at history, that those who are remembered for achieving greatness seemed to be lone warriors?" Jesus Christ never married. Buddha was single. The public never heard about Albert Einstein's wife. Henry David Thoreau went to Walden alone.

"I think we are in the middle of a huge transition," Hendricks replied. "If you look at the time of Jesus, Buddha, and Thoreau, it was an era of the male hero in which God was viewed as a man. If you went back 5,000-10,000 years before the male era there was also a time of female heroes with the Goddess. But now what I think is going on is it's not the male or the female that is the hero. It's the relationship itself that is the hero."

Perhaps the Hendricks are right. Maybe the reason we think lone warriors are more successful is because history doesn't acknowledge the contribution of their partners. I know many women who would agree. As one office poster states, "Behind every great man is a woman and behind every great woman is herself!"

So if history has lied to us and great men and women have really achieved their accomplishments *because* of relationships and not *in spite* of relationships, what then is the secret to making a relationship and one's individual dreams work together?

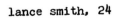

lance smith, 24

nickname:
claysmile

hometown:
silver spring, md

favorite food:
chinese food

biggest concern:
the spiritual
health of our
world

favorite song:
beautiful day by
u2

life motto: to
god be the glory!

read more of
what lance had
to share in
"how can i make
money?" and
visit his website
claysmile.com

The key is to quit playing games with yourself. Relationships are made into scapegoats. Every single one of us has a tendency to procrastinate. When we have no one to blame for not getting a project complete, we tend just to let it slide. But when we are in a relationship, we quickly tag the blame onto the relationship.

Picture in your mind two guys, Bill and Ted, on a lunch break at work. It's Monday and Bill is unwrapping his sandwich. "Oh, no, it's peanut butter and jelly! My wife is going to hear about this," cries out Bill, as he looks inside the wrapper.

The next day Bill and Ted are again at the table eating their lunches. Bill pulls back the wrapper of his sandwich. "Peanut butter and jelly *again*! Oh she's never going to get it. Am I doomed to forever dine on peanut butter and jelly?" whines Bill, as Ted rolls his eyes.

Wednesday comes and again Bill complains about his lunch of peanut butter and jelly. When Thursday arrives Ted is thinking about sitting somewhere else but decides to give Bill another chance. Once more Bill pulls back the wrapper to expose a peanut butter and jelly sandwich. As he starts to complain Ted yells out, "Bill, every day you complain about the peanut butter and jelly! I am tired of all your complaining! Why don't you ask your wife to fix you a different sandwich?"

Bill looked at Ted with a confused look and then calmly stated, "Ted, my wife doesn't fix my lunch. I fix my lunch every morning!"

While ridiculous, the point of the story is that we often pass blame on someone else when it's truly our own doing. Think about it. How many times have you said, "Yeah, I'd like to participate, but the lady won't approve," or, "If I didn't have to keep track of his life, I'd have so much more time to work on my own business." The truth is, and I'm speaking from experience, that we have plenty of time to be in a relationship and to accomplish our individual goals. No relationship has the power to take you away from your dreams unless you give it power. Unfortunately, we

trick ourselves into believing our relationship is the reason we're not achieving our goals instead of our own lack of focus.

Opportunity

You can be in a relationship and achieve your individual goals. In fact, it's the only way to be truly successful. The key is not to blame your lack of success on the relationship, but to look honestly at how you are investing your life.

Each of us, no matter the color of our skin, the language we speak, or the type of car we drive has 24 hours in a day. The following exercise is great way to become aware and accountable for where you are dedicating your time.

Put down the number of hours you normally invest in one day for each of the categories below. You will notice two columns; one is for how you spend your time during the weekdays and the other is for the weekend *(see following page)*.

Dedicating your Time

Weekday Weekend

1. Career, work, and business

2. Relationship with your partner

3. Health and fitness

4. Personal growth and development

5. Social and community activities

6. Family and friends

7. Leisure and relaxation

8. Doing nothing but thinking about doing something

Look closely at the number of hours you devote to each area. Are you surprised? Chances are that you'll discover you're not investing *enough* time into your relationship instead of *too much* time. Instead of avoiding a relationship, clean up the other areas of your life where you are wasting time.

CHAPTER TWENTY-FOUR

Should I go for the big bucks or pursue what I truly want to do?

Did you hear about the asteroid? According to astronomers, the world as we know it could end on March 21, 2014. Scientists have discovered a giant mass of stone and space debris that may strike the Earth with a force so powerful it destroys our planet in an instant. A spokesman for the British government reported, "On impact, it could have the effect of 20 million Hiroshima atomic bombs."

Now, before you get too worried, let me inform you that the chances of a collision are less than 1 in 909,000. But let's imagine for a moment that the world is coming to an end. What then? Your savings account, retirement fund, and big house payments seem a lot less important. Right? Whereas your relationships and the quality of

your remaining time become very important.

I'm the first to admit that it's easy to see the value of your dreams and relationships when your life is cut short. But what about when you have 30, 40, 50, or 60 years of your life remaining?

Po Bronson, author of *What Should I Do with My Life?*, taught me about the lockbox theory of life. In interviewing over 900 people for his book, he discovered that some people put their dreams aside as if in storage. They then go out and try to make lots of #!$*% money, planning to return to their dreams after becoming financially secure.

When I asked Bronson how many of the people he'd interviewed, who put their dreams away in a lockbox,

wendy hitt, 22

hometown:
blue bell, pa

favorite movie:
the neverending story

biggest concern:
that our generation grows up not really happy with life and teaches our children this

what you wish you knew two years ago: that things change...answers are there...and life goes on...

life motto:
experience everything possible then laugh or cry your way home

had successfully opened it up later in their lives, he said none of the people were able to go back and reclaim the dreams they had locked away when they decided to pursue the big bucks. In other words, they got distracted and never came back to those dreams that they'd tucked away so many years ago. It seems that the lockbox theory may be best kept as a theory and not a practice.

John, a 27-year-old music director, grew up in a wealthy family. When it came time to decide on a college degree, he had a major decision to make. His family wanted him to go into medicine, law, or another lucrative profession. But John chose a different route. He chose to major in music. I asked him why he made the decision.

"Well, part of it was the thrill, the adolescent defiance of shaking my fists at my parents and saying, 'You can't tell me what to do!' " said John. "Another part of it was that I had some magnificent professors in the music department at college, whom I trusted very much. My first year there, I took a couple of music courses simply because I thought it would be something I would do on the side. I found I enjoyed the classes, the assignments, and putting in the work. I thought to myself, 'I could spend my whole life doing something that I don't enjoy and wondering if I could do this, or I could do this now.' And I did it."

One of the biggest challenges for John in deciding on his career in music was the obvious drop in financial status from the level to which he was accustomed. "There was a brief moment when I came out of college when it really hit me that I wasn't going to make a whole lot of money," said John. "Having grown up in money, it really was a blow to the face. But that feeling didn't last too long. I think, in part, the reason it never really got to me was because I was a little untrustworthy of the attitudes in which I had grown up. If you grow up poor you want to be rich, and if you grow up rich you can easily get caught in the rat race." It has been several years now, and John still is thankful for his decision to follow his dreams instead of his bank account.

One of my favorite quotes is taken from Mary Kay Ash, the founder of Mary Kay Cosmetics, who said, "Don't die with your music still in you." For several years, I volunteered with Hospice of the Twin Cities in Minneapolis, Minnesota. There I spent time with individuals who weren't expected to live more than three months. I remember the pain and sadness that a man named Bill expressed when he reflected back over his life. "I always wanted to fly an airplane, but didn't pursue it," he told me one afternoon. Although he'd lived over seven decades, he was full of regret and disappointment for the things he never ventured to do. As another woman in hospice told me, "Jason, you won't regret the things you did, but you will regret the things you didn't do."

A key to living a fulfilling life is to stay aware of how short and precious life is. Do you know how many Sundays the average person has in her/his lifetime? There are 4,264 Sundays in an 82 year life span.

adam hatman, 18

favorite food: munchies

biggest concern: the drug laws

best date advice: don't go home with her if she don't got no teeth

what you wish you knew two years ago: none of my ex-girlfriends

life motto: try to live up to your name

Did you realize the following?

An 19-year-old has used 936 Sundays or 22 percent of her/his life supply.

A 25-year-old has used 1,248 Sundays or 29 percent of her/his life supply.

A 35-year-old has used 1,768 Sundays or 41 percent of her/his life supply.

Keep in mind this refers to an 82 year life span. Unfortunately life can be taken from us at any time. Accidents, illness, and war can all claim your life tomorrow. Pursue something you care about and make today count, because you cannot count on tomorrow!

Opportunity

One way to remind yourself of the shortness of life is to use a jar of marbles. What you will need for this activity is a glass or plastic jar, marbles, and the quick use of a math formula.

Big bucks or not...

Step One—The Formula:

To begin with take your current age and subtract it from 82. For example if you are 25 the answer would be 82 – 25 = 57. The second step is to take your answer (i.e., 57) and multiply it by 12, the number of months in a year. 57 x 12 = 684. This is roughly the number of months you have remaining in your lifetime.

Step Two—Marbles:

Take the number of years you have remaining in your lifetime and purchase that many marbles. Hint: you may instead chose to purchase balls of gum, hard candy, or even BBs if you like.

Step Three—The Jar:

Fill a jar with the marbles or candy. It is a good idea to label the jar. For example you may call it, "Your Earthly Parking Meter" or "My Time Remaining." The purpose of labeling it is not to be morbid, rather to remind you of the preciousness of your life.

Place a label on the lid with the question: *Am I pursuing what I truly want to do?* Once the jar is labeled, I recommend that you place this jar in an area where you will regularly see it.

Step Four—The Process:

On the first day of each month take out one of the marbles or pieces of candy from your jar. When you do this it reminds you that your life is passing by. You will be prompted to reflect on the question: *Am I pursuing what I truly want to do?* This is a great reminder to keep you on the right track.

157

WHERE ARE YOU FROM
Coral Springs, Florida

WHERE TO YOU LIVE NOW
Denver, CO

FAVORITE FOOD
stuffed shells

FAVORITE SONG
♪♪ ♪♪

BIGGEST CONCERN AS A QUARTERLIFER
Not being able to survive financially

LAST BOOK YOU READ
Pledged

FAVORITE MOVIE

BEST DATE ADVICE
e yourself like friends so you not nervous

WORST DATE ADVICE

SECRET TO LIFE

FINAL THOUGHT?
World

Age 2

Job → Fin
Mature

How many Jobs
year → 4 = our
temp

Biggest Loser
→ Be positive & never give
keep push like the first da

Δ in generation
like want to be financial
stable & create a career
ourselves instead of just
married & becoming a h
wife,

to make a living & prove yourself to everyone
at the same time trying yourself & Staying the

CHAPTER TWENTY-FIVE

How can I make money?

Shortly after midnight, hundreds of treasure hunters climbed over fallen trees and dug through fresh snow in search of a small, plastic medallion. "How can you dig?" questioned 20-year-old Ryan, who for the past three nights had been searching until 3 A.M. "There are too many people. I don't think 'nuts' describes the situation."

Thousands of people brave sub-zero wind chills to join the search as part of the annual St. Paul Winter Carnival. The medallion is always hidden on public property, and new clues to its location are issued daily in the *St. Paul Pioneer Press*. Serious seekers line up each evening at the newspaper's main office to buy early editions, and then dial out the latest clues by cell phone to their partners in the field. Some people even take vacation days from work to search full-time, whereas others, such as recent winners Virginia and Luis Ibarra, wait until their children leave for school each day before they join the hunt.

A few hours after the release of the 12th clue, which described a wildflower sign and included the statement, "50 large paces, you're off to the races," Virginia and Luis uncovered the medallion after only 10 minutes of searching. "We just started scraping and there it was," said Luis.

Why would people take weeks off from their paying jobs to search for a medallion? Why would they put up with sub-zero wind chills and crowds of people? They do it for the same reason that tens of thousands of people audition for *American Idol,* the same reason that Ed McMahon was able to build his Publisher's Clearing House fortune, the same reason people agree to be

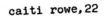

caiti rowe, 22

hometown: coral spring, fl

biggest concern: not being able to survive financially

number of jobs in the last year: four

difference between our generation and our parents: we want to be financially stable and create a career for ourselves instead of just getting married and becoming housewives

life motto: keep on pushing like the first day

contestants on TV programs like *Fear Factor, Survivor,* and *Who Wants to Be a Millionaire,* and for the same reason they buy lottery tickets. They do it for the dream of sudden cold cash. The medallion is worth $10,000 to the winner.

We witness an 18-year-old high school basketball player, Lebron James, signing a $90 million contract with Nike. We hear that promoters guaranteed Britney Spears, age 21, an income of $200,000 per show on her 100-stop tour, and can only imagine her vast income from record sales, sponsors, and products. Did you know that the Britney doll netted over $15 million in a single year? Then there are computer geniuses, like Michael Dell and Jeff Bezos, who started amassing billion dollar fortunes in their 20s. Is it any wonder that during a series of street interviews on the 16th Street Mall in Denver, Colorado, the majority of 20-year-olds told me they planned to retire in one to ten years?

When I asked these quarterlifers how they planned on having enough money to retire before age 40, the top 3 most common responses were, "I'm going to win the lottery," "I'll become a rock star," and, "I'll play professional sports."

In reality, few of us will win the Powerball, sing at the Shoreline, or play in the Superbowl. Once you accept this truth, then you can address the underlying issue: How can I make money? Every morning your computer inbox is filled with junk email promising easy ways to make thousands of dollars from the comfort of your home. Late night TV infomercials offer real estate and investing kits for purchase. Community colleges and vocational schools flood the radio airwaves with new and lucrative career paths to follow. Lawyer ads decorate bus stop benches asking you to use their services because they squeeze the money from insurance companies better than anyone else. So, what is the best way to make money?

The first step is that you must have the desire to make money. Many people think that money is the root of evil. If you believe this, you will continually sabotage your efforts, just as a new groom who

believes marriage is nothing more than a low-security prison reduces his chance of having a happy marriage. Without desire, it won't work! When Wall Street investment legend Ace Greenberg was recently asked, amidst a room of Fairfield University business students, what he looks for in the elite people he hires, he flatly stated, "We don't hold it against people who have advanced degrees, like MBAs, but we do prefer people with PSDs: poor, smart, and a deep desire to become rich."

This is the same characteristic that Napoleon Hill, author of the classic *Think and Grow Rich,* found central to the wealthiest individuals of the mid-1900s. Hill invested 20 years interviewing and studying the likes of Andrew Carnegie, J. P. Morgan, and Henry Ford. After two decades of research, he reached the conclusion, "The starting point of all achievement is desire. Keep this constantly in mind. Weak desire brings weak results, just as a small amount of fire makes a small amount of heat."

ben rouse, 23

hometown:
sioux city, ia

favorite food:
pancakes with
strawberry syrup

biggest concern:
that my pursuit
for a good
career rather
than a basic job
will limit my
relationship with
my son since i
can't find work
in sioux city, ia

favorite tv show:
boston legal

best date advice:
relax and be
yourself

life motto:
whatever you
choose to do, do
your best

Once you have the desire to make money, the next step is to find a field that incites your passion. Lance Smith, 24, also known as Claysmile, has built a successful speaking and performing career while pursuing undergraduate studies at the University of Maryland. "It's my passion. I believe that this is really what I want to do," Claysmile told me about his speaking career. "I want to make this work. When I'm presenting it's so fulfilling that I don't see any other way." Claysmile receives up to $3,500 for his talks, because people are willing to pay once they can see how much he cares.

"The bottom line has to do with where you focus your attention," Maria Nemeth, former clinical professor in the Department of Psychiatry at the University of California-Davis School of Medicine and author of *The Energy of Money*, told me. "Are you focusing it upon what has real meaning for you? Or are you focusing on simply getting more because you're afraid of getting less?" This is one of the solutions. I think we can do anything to make money in the short-term, but to make big money and be satisfied over the long-term, we must focus on doing what we love. This doesn't mean it will always be easy, instead we will have the drive to move forward even when it is rough.

The willingness to roll up your sleeves and work is the third step in making money. The universe does not give something for nothing. As Napoleon Hill observed, "The path of least resistance makes all rivers, and some men, crooked."

Understanding the importance of focused work, Claysmile took a semester off from college to devote his days fully to building a speaking career. "I wanted to clear my plate, so I could focus on speaking and build a base I could really expand." Like Lance, your desire and pursuit of a passion is the most powerful tool you have for making money. When you find pleasure in mastering your expertise and are able to pick yourself up after each setback then you create an unstoppable momentum.

How could anyone reach excellence and command top dollar if he or she didn't have a passion driving him or her forward? With desire and passion, your work becomes your play and it is easy to invest your time, energy, and soul. Without that driving force, you will quickly be surpassed by those who possess it.

The good news is that in the United States we live in one of the ripest times and places in history to make money. Today, as glass ceilings and walls of limitation crumble down, you and I have opportunities about which our parents only dreamed. As 20- and 30-year-olds, we are in prime position to succeed, because we have the energy reserves necessary to pursue our passions. I repeatedly hear older clients in my chiropractic office say they wish they still had the endurance they had fresh out of college.

Unfortunately, these two decades are also the age when many of us get derailed by drug abuse, meaningless sex, endless barhopping, and television marathons. This is the double-edged sword of youth. We

megan eggers, 28

where you live:
boulder, co

biggest concern:
the state of
disembodiment
of the general
public, from
our bodies,
our spirits,
and our sense
of community.
i see people
disconnected from
their life-force
and mindlessly
seeking anything
for a feeling of
connection.

favorite movie:
the nature
outside my door

life motto:
breathe

have abundant energy but often use it frivolously. The solution is to channel the energy of our youth towards that which we love and that which we are destined to do.

Opportunity

The American Dream is alive and well for anyone willing to role up their sleeves and pursue their desire. The following three steps will help you discover and develop that fierce passion.

To begin, you must have a desire to make money. As long as you think it is noble and spiritual to live in poverty you will have trouble making money. To cultivate desire, write out 100 answers to the following question: *When I am wealthy, what will I do with the money?* In the process, you may discover that you would establish a home for abused children, write a book, take your family to Europe, sponsor a community art festival, buy an Alaskan cruise for your parents, or move to a house overlooking the Pacific Ocean. When you link making money with the realization of your dreams, it fuels the fire of desire to have income.

Next, recognize your passion. Discover this by answering the question: *If I could do anything in the universe and be beautifully/handsomely paid for it, what would it be?* Resist your temptation to squelch ideas because they don't seem practical or possible. Instead, write down the first thing that comes to mind, and then the next, and so on. Once you have completed a page or two, pick out your top choice, the single item you would like to pursue above the others.

The final step is to ask *What resources are available? To whom do I need to talk? And, what do I need to do to begin making money doing _____ (the passion you highlighted above)?* These questions reveal your action steps.

A sign that you are on the right track is that the pursuit of your passion takes on a life of its own. You will find it motivating and fulfilling to earn income this way and always keep in mind what American financial analyst, Charles

more from megan...

favorite book- my journal, when i can get there

best date advice: share as much of yourself as possible, be vulnerable, and let your heart be seen

worst date advice: go in thinking that you have to do something/anything to change who you are to be loved or accepted

what you wish you knew two years ago: that what i was doing then would get me here now

secret to life: the secret is to enjoy the little things in life. that is where the spirit of life lives.

read more of what megan had to share in "what should i do for a living?"

Schwab once said, "The man who does not work for the love of work but only for money is not likely to make money nor find much fun in life."

nick farber, 25

hometown:
reno, nv

occupation: law student

biggest concern:
how much money i'm going to make in four years

last read: basic tort law

best date advice:
plan ahead, remember key dates, but stay unpredictable

secret to life:
things happen for a reason; learn to go with the flow

final thought:
age doesn't matter after 21

CHAPTER TWENTY-SIX

Where should I invest my money?

"Get your slice of the moon! Come one, come all, get your lunar plot." This is no joke! An Australian real estate agency, Lunar Realty, is selling one-acre and ten-acre lots on the moon.

It all began back in 1980 when Nevada entrepreneur Dennis Hope claimed to have found loopholes in the 1967 United Nations Outer Space Treaty, which prevented nations from claiming the moon, but said nothing about individuals having ownership.

Dennis sent letters to the United States, Soviet Union, and the United Nations announcing his registration of the moon and has been selling lots ever since. After selling lunar lots to over 2 million people from 180 countries Dennis recently sold the company to a 33-year-old Australian, Paul Jackson, who founded Lunar Realty.

Paul is selling the one-acre blocks for $40 and the ten-acre blocks for $298. He even bought a lot for himself saying, "I would be extremely happy if one day we got the chance to live on the moon. I look at the world around us and think stranger things have happened."

While strange things do happen, investing in extraterrestrial real estate is probably not high on your list. There are, however, plenty of difficult decisions when it comes to investing money. Do you put your money in the stock market, a home, your business, an education, savings, a car, or stuff it under the mattress? What is the difference between bonds, mutual funds, the money

rebecca williams, 25

occupation: sales

biggest concern: wondering if it will all work out—job, family, life goals, finances, etc.

favorite movie: gladiator

worst date advice: dating someone you met at last call

what to look for in a leader: someone who leads by example, listens, is honest, and doesn't ignore problems, but works to solve them

market, stocks, a tax lien, and the S&P? How much money do you need to get started in investing? Should you begin investing now or should you first pay off all your debts? These are just a few of the many overwhelming questions that arise when deciding where to put your money.

I find it interesting that we are taught how to read, write, and communicate in school; how to drive in driver's education; how to shoot and handle a gun in hunter's safety course; and how to have safe sex in gym class, yet most of us have never been taught how to handle money. In fact, even when I filed my chiropractic office as a corporation, the state did not test to see if I knew the basics about money. Did you realize that only four states require that high school students take a personal finance course in order to graduate?

I asked Chris, a 27-year-old financial advisor in South Dakota, how he approaches his money and investing. "You should have priorities," he told me. "The first priority is a house. The second priority, especially if you have a family, is protection. You need to have a minimal amount of life insurance or money in a safe investment so if something happens there is money there to take care of what needs to be taken care of."

"Any money after that I personally think should go into the stock market. If you're young most of it should go into a high risk fund. As you get older you should put more in secure investments."

Chris continued, "It depends on your personality, too. For example my wife and I have some of our money in reasonably safe investments and some in high risk investments. For me it's fun to follow the high risk and to play around with it. I enjoy changing the investment to this or that, but some people don't have a tolerance for that risk. They should probably invest in safe investments for the peace of mind. If you put it in the stock market you can put it in safe investments that are reasonably assured to make 6-8 percent a year for 30-40 years, and 6 percent is about twice inflation.

"Also, if possible, you should invest in a business. Maybe more so than the stock market. Not everyone can do that, but if you have the money, ambition, or idea and your business does well you can obviously make more than 12 percent a year, which is greater than what you may do in the stock market."

Chris and his wife, Kelli, have established a solid financial foundation. They have been able to do this because they are what Robert Allen, a self-made multi-millionaire and author of the *One Minute Millionaire*, calls financially literate. They understand how money works and how to make it grow.

Unfortunately Chris and Kelli are the exception. Most of us have little knowledge or experience with investing money. In fact one of the common patterns I found while conducting research interviews for this book is that our generation spends money when we have it and charges it when we don't. Did you realize that in the United States the total debt of individuals is $9.2 trillion, which exceeds the national

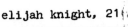

elijah knight, 21

favorite food:
mexican/spanish

biggest concern:
money

favorite movie:
friday

best date advice:
worry about
yourself

life motto: if i
don't focus up,
i won't get no
bottom line

debt? We complain about the government's expenditures, and yet many of us are doing the same thing with our own credit cards.

Larry A. Voorhees, a National Sales Director with Primerica Financial Services, told me, "What's happening is that we are living in a microwave society. Everybody wants it hot, fast, and now. They plan more for a two-week vacation than they do for their retirement. People need to sit down and look at what they need to do with their money. People need a plan. It really doesn't take a whole lot to get that million or two million if you let time work for you. The key to being financially independent is understanding the fundamentals of finances and money."

These fundamentals are the ones Chris understands and the ones Allen means when he says become financially literate. **The secret to investing is learning and applying the fundamentals.** They include Benjamin Franklin's Rule of 72, which states if you take the percent interest you are earning and divide it into the number 72 that is the number of years it will take for your money to double. For example if you are receiving 12 percent on an investment it will take 6 years for your money to double.

Another fundamental is the Rule of Compound Interest and Time. As 20- and 30-year-olds we have an advantage our parents and grandparents will never have again—time. Did you know that if you invested a dollar a day with 10 percent interest you will be a millionaire in 56 years?

A third fundamental is to Pay Yourself First. From books like *The Richest Man in Babylon* to the financial leaders on television, a common mantra is to immediately take 10 percent of your pay check and invest it. Otherwise it is easy to blow through it and have more days than money left at the end of each month.

These fundamentals are like a recipe for baking a cake. The closer you stick to them the greater the chance that you will get the outcome you want.

Opportunity

Money is a part of all our lives. We earn it, spend it, save it, and invest it. The greater our knowledge about money the better our chances of creating more of it. The key is to enroll personally in a financial education. The following are resources and books that I recommend to quicken your learning curve.

The Richest Man in Babylon by George S. Clason

The 24 Essential Lessons for Investment Success by William J. O'Neil

Rich Dad, Poor Dad by Robert T. Kiyosaki

The One Minute Millionaire by Robert Allen and Mark Victor Hansen

The Millionaire Next Door by Thomas Stanley and William Danko

It can also be valuable to sit down with a financial advisor to discuss your situation. This may be the easiest way to get started. As one certified financial analyst I've sought

sara dykstra, 28

hometown: grand rapids, mi

current job: peace corps in grenada

biggest concern: currently, it's helping grenada get back on its feet after a hurricane

what you wish you knew two years ago: when you feel you want to take the road less traveled for a while...just do it

life motto: dwell in possibility

read more of what sara had to share in "what is the real world?"

advice from, told me, "Working with 20- and 30-year-olds is fun and relatively straight forward. The best part is that they can apply good financial practices from the beginning without making all the mistakes that their parents did."

Please visit

www.UploadExperience.com

and click on *Financial Resources* for

a list of financial advisors.

CHAPTER TWENTY-SEVEN

Should I travel and explore before settling down?

"It's amazing the gentleman survived. It's a bizarre case," said Lori Bailey, an FBI Special Agent.

Officials were baffled when Charles McKinley, 25, shipped himself in a cargo crate from his home in New York to his parents' home in Dallas. After spending over 12 hours in the crate Charles pried himself free, leapt out of the crate, shook the hand of the deliveryman, and walked up to his parents' doorstep! He was later arrested.

While it was downright stupid and dangerous for Charles to ship himself to Texas, the truth is that for a few bucks you and I can easily travel the globe. Greyhound and Amtrak will take us around the United States and we can fly the friendly skies anywhere in the world we want. Today it's not a question of *can* we travel, instead it's a question of *should* we travel and explore before settling down in the real world?

Ted Kerosote, author of *Out There in the Wild in a Wired Age* and a regular writer for *Outside Magazine*, told me he thinks it's wise to travel and explore before settling down. "I spent a year and a half, when I got out of college, traveling in Central and South America," said Kerosote. "That was just as important, perhaps more important, than the graduate school I eventually went to. It was my graduate school in life, and I think that unfortunately too many folks simply go from high school to college to the workplace without ever taking time off to see how the real world works."

jason dorsey, 24

hometown:
austin, tx

favorite food:
sushi

biggest concern:
developing the
next generation
of leaders

favorite movie:
dead poets
society

**most likely place
to visit:** coffee
shop

life motto:
anything is
possible

read more of
what jason had
to share in "is
life fair?" and
visit his website
jasondorsey.com

Kerosote continued, "Not only did I travel in Central and South America, I also spent a lot of time in Asia and Africa. One quickly realizes that other people in the world do things differently. They conduct their family relationships differently. They conduct politics differently. They conduct their day-to-day life with different rhythms and different emphasis. Through traveling, I began to see that the North American way of doing things was not the only way. We don't have the corner on doing things the right way. That experience has allowed me to develop humility and compromise more readily with other folks rather than saying this is the one and only way."

Kerosote makes two important points. First, traveling can provide an education that far exceeds that of formal schooling. Too often we forget that school is not the end, but a means to an end. Remember the adage, "Don't let school get in the way of your education."

The second point that deserves attention is that Kerosote's entire life changed when he began to see the world from the eyes of others. I really think this is the key point. It's not a question of whether one should travel before settling down, but instead it's a question of how can one gain insight into his or her own life before becoming locked into one way of seeing the world. For many, this insight comes through traveling and experiencing new places, people, and events. For others, it may come through conversations that occur in your own town with people from different backgrounds and cultures. Finally, some gain this insight by reading the life stories of a variety of people and places. **Regardless of how you do it, I believe it's critical that each of us expand our perspective before settling down in the real world.**

For Jamie, 18, this expansion began early when she began modeling. "It happened suddenly. I was 16 and in my junior year of high school. After my braces were removed everyone kept telling me that I should model. So, I went to an audition and two weeks later I was in Italy on my first shoot," she told me.

Since that first job, Jamie has lived and worked in Tokyo, Singapore, New York, Miami, Barcelona, Paris, and Los Angeles. "I think it's good to travel. It's made me more aware of what I want from life. I've had good and bad experiences that have made me grow. I have a better understanding of what I want and when I want it."

While Jamie is actively seeking new experiences and adventures, she has friends who are not. "One of my close friends is the exact opposite," she told me. "He has his little box that he stays in. He's graduating from college and likes being settled. He's lived in the same house, been with the same girlfriend, and hangs out with the same friends. He says he's just fine, but I don't think he's ever really looked at life outside of the one he knows."

Recently I attended my ten year high school reunion. It wasn't long ago when the reunion seemed like a distant date on the calendar. (How the years fly by!) As I talked with old classmates on the first evening it really struck me. More than what degree someone earned, where they

alyssa woods, 19

favorite food: any kind of fruit

biggest concern: getting through college with as little financial stress as possible

last read: challenges of politics

what you wish you knew two years ago: that you can't live life being afraid. you will miss a lot of opportunities that way.

life motto: to be happy and successful in everything i do

lived, or how many children they had, what stood out was how they viewed the world. For some the world was the same today as it was ten years ago—the same problems, complaints, and opinions. But for others, they saw the world with completely new eyes, and it showed.

Logan, a former classmate who's now a computer training consultant, has traveled to over 36 countries since graduating. Many of these trips were business related and involved living and working in countries for months at a time. Noticing a significant change in Logan at our reunion, I asked him what role travel has played in shaping who he is today. "The personal friendships I have made from traveling and working abroad have had the largest impact on me," he said. "Faceless, far off places suddenly have new meaning, when I have a friend there. I definitely am much better educated about other countries, people, ways of living, different forms of architecture, art, and food—the food may be the best part of traveling! It has helped me understand and appreciate my own culture and country better. With the things I've seen and done it's harder to surprise me now than ten years ago. I'm much more open to new ideas, and appreciate originality, while at the same time, I've solidified many of my own principles and beliefs and can better filter what things are worthwhile and what things are frivolous. Above all, I am much more confident in myself and my abilities. I could be dropped off in the middle of nearly any city, and feel that I could get around and make a way for myself."

It's said that the only difference between a rut and a grave is the depth and length of time we spend there. We begin digging our graves in our 20s when we fail to expand our perspective of the world. No longer do you and I live in a world that is untouched by people of neighboring towns, states, or countries. Instead, every day we come in contact with the cultures of others. Just pick up the phone and call tech support for your computer. Chances are you'll be talking to

someone in India or the Philippines. Turn on the television and there are shows being broadcast in Spanish, German, and French. Today's world is one community and the only way to be a participating member is by expanding one's views to understand those of other members of the global community.

Opportunity

Today you don't have to choose between exploring and settling down. There are many constructive ways to travel that also further one's expertise and skills. You may chose to do a semester abroad while in high school or college. It's even possible to do a semester at sea—traveling the world in a cruise ship and taking college courses on board. Once you leave college there are countless jobs that involve travel. Like Logan, you may find yourself working your way up the corporate ladder and at the same time visiting distant states and countries.

There is no easier time in history to travel the globe than right now. But traveling in and of itself is not the answer. The key is to make your

brandon boaturght, 21

favorite place to visit: amsterdam

last read: huxley and god by aldous huxley

biggest concern: the existential dilemma of mankind

favorite food: anything

best date advice: learn to love yourself

secret to life: there is no secret to life. there is no answer. life is what you make of it. you should never rest your mind on any idea. never stop searching.

travels a way of expanding your understanding of the world.

Regardless of why you are traveling, here are three steps you can take to expand your perspective as you go.

1. Learn the history of the area. It's amazing how people, places, and things come alive when you first know their history.

2. When in Rome, do as the Romans do. Take in the local culture. If you're fortunate to have a town fair, concert, or special event occur during your visit, be sure to take it in. Observing how the locals interact and celebrate will certainly teach you a great deal about their ways and your own.

3. Get lost. Guided tours are great but to truly experience new people and places you need to explore, investigate, question, and discover on your own. You'll be amazed at the people you meet and the places they show you when you first show an interest in them.

Remember the words of author Roger Dawson, as you travel and experience the world. He said,

"Our world exists only through our perception of it. Change our perception of our world and we change the world—for us."

more from brandon...

favorite movie: waking life

difference between our generation and our parents: we are human beings living in a complex world beyond our comprehension. my generation seems to be coming to the understanding that there is more to life than is represented to us.

final thought: think and try to understand as much as you can. never stop searching.

read brandon's full discourse on page 26

life is what you make it. there is no secret

AGE — 29

HOMETOWN Bailey, CO

WHERE YOU LIVE NOW In and around Bailey, Front Range CO, seasonally on Western Slope, Colo.

FAVORITE FOOD Traditional Mexican dishes / Seafood ~~anything~~ Anything with Avacados

BIGGEST CONCERN

Getting stuck in a routine that I can't get out of, and not getting to ~~experience~~ experience enough of the exotic & foriegn

FAVORITE MOVIE

"A Fish Called Wanda"

BEST DATE ADVICE

"Learn to cook, a man who cooks well will never be hungry or alone."

WORST DATE ADVICE

That double dates are a good idea, ~~especially~~ especially to cigar bars.

LIFE MOTTO

Keep your eye on the cookie or

A rolling stone gathers no moss

WHAT YOU WISH YOU WOULD HAVE KNOWN TWO YEARS AGO

~~You~~ You don't even know what stress is, until you have kids who drive.
                    ∧
            or stepkids

FAVORITE ~~MOVIE~~ Book

"Pillars of the Earth" by Ken Follett

2nd choice Pigmallion by Shaw

CHAPTER TWENTY-EIGHT

Where should I live?

How far did you travel today? Five miles? Twenty miles? Maybe you're on a plane right now traveling hundreds of miles from the bed you woke up in. Now imagine if you never traveled more than 37 miles from your home during your entire lifetime. Hmm, pretty limiting, isn't it?

This was the reality for Oetzi, a 5,200-year-old Iceman who was found in the mountains of northern Italy. "Our data indicates that the Iceman spent his entire life in the immediate area," said a team of researchers studying elements in Oetzi's teeth and bones. When you've only traveled a total of 37 miles from your home, deciding where to live is not a big deal. You and I, on the other hand have a much greater decision to make. Once we step out into the real world we have to decide where in the *world* to call home.

Settling on where to live is one of the most important decisions you'll make starting out in life. The values, opportunities, and climate of the people and places around you can shape the person you become. Isn't it ironic that you spend days trying to find the right apartment to rent or months trying to find the right home to buy, but you often choose where to live on a whim?

I'll never forget how Brian, a high school friend, made his decision. One night a couple of years back we were hanging out before going to the bars. Bored, Brian was flipping through a road atlas and reading the featured articles on towns in the United States. A few paragraphs into a page he raised his head and calmly told me, "I am going to get out of here and move to Bend, Oregon." I remember thinking *Yeah, whatever. Just finish your beer*

katie watts, 34

hometown:
ft. smith, ar

favorite food:
pizza

biggest concern:
making enough
money to support
myself

best date advice:
don't take your
date to a loud
club on the first
date

life motto: just
be!

and let's go downtown. Two months later, Brian packed up his Chevy Blazer, tied his mattress to the top, and left his parents' home for the first time.

Recently I asked Brian why he decided to move to Oregon back then. "It wasn't that I was searching for the right city. I was just looking for something different from what I knew," he told me. "Everything got so routine. I was doing things I didn't want to do because I didn't have other options. When I moved, it was a fresh start. I could do whatever I wanted to do."

Like Brian, many quarterlifers move to a new city hungry to start fresh. They are less concerned about where they *move to* than what they are *moving away from.* It's no surprise. As quarterlifers we've been conditioned to expect change. From the time we finish high school to the time we start our first job, we move on average once every three months. In fact, we become so conditioned to moving that for years after college graduation many quarterlifers still talk about feeling the urgency to pick up and go each spring and fall.

Where should I live?

While many in our generation are randomly deciding where to live, others are looking more closely at the question. "It was important to be close to my family," Carrie, a 23-year-old fitness trainer, told me. "I've lived close to family and I've lived far away. I like being close better. Plus, I want to have children in the future and believe it's important for children to know their grandparents as they grow up."

The key to deciding where to live is to reflect on what's most important to you and at the same time, to be open to new possibilities in your life. Take the time to sit down and look at what you want right now. Start by examining your current priorities. What are your interests? Ultimately, you have to live somewhere. Why not make a conscious decision where it will be? Even in the worst case scenario that you make a decision and dislike it, you're still better off than not having made a conscious decision in the first place.

Once you've gained insight into what you truly desire, the next step is to be open to what comes into your life. Something magical occurs when you open up and go with the flow. As Oriah Mountain Dreamer, the gifted writer of *The Invitation* and *The Call*, told me, "When you let go of wanting things to be a certain way, when you let go of your certainty that you know how things should be, you find yourself letting go of resisting or resenting what is true in this moment. And in this acceptance you become a conscious participant in a larger flow."

I agree with Oriah. In my own life, I experienced this flow four years ago as I graduated from chiropractic college and was trying to decide where to live. At the time I wrote out all the qualities that I desired in a hometown. The list included being in or next to mountains, located near a major interstate highway, having access to hiking trails within five minutes of town, a large enough population base to support a chiropractic practice, and being close enough to a major airport that I could be there in an hour, among others. Taking my list of qualities, I pinpointed towns in Colorado, California,

matt johnson, 23

hometown: north wilkesboro, nc

biggest concern: our country is falling away from what it was founded on

secret to life: knowing your purpose

difference between our generation and our parents: our generation works less and tries to gain more while our parents worked harder just to get by

life motto: live life outside your comfort zone. live on the edge.

Idaho, and Nevada that had all or a majority of the qualities I desired. Then I loaded up my vehicle and drove to Colorado—my first stop. This is where the magic began. As I was going from town to town, a major snowstorm hit the Rockies and led me to pull off the road for the night in a town called Idaho Springs, instead of driving to Ft. Collins, as I had planned.

The next morning, the storm had passed and the sun came out highlighting a winter wonderland. It was truly one of those moments John Denver called having a "Rocky Mountain high." I decided that instead of rushing to Ft. Collins, I would take a detour and visit the nearby town of Evergreen and see if I could find a hiking trail. (By the way, I had originally considered visiting Evergreen, but had crossed it off of my list before the trip.) That morning as I drove into Evergreen, not only did I find a place to hike I found a place to live. I made my decision in the first 20 minutes and now, 4 years later, I still feel blessed to be here. Ironically, as I write these words my home office is only yards away from the trail that I hiked that first day.

Here's the point. While I did carefully craft a list of qualities I desired in a place to live, ultimately it was a snowstorm and the spontaneous idea of going for a hike that led me to where I live today. I do think that I was able to *recognize* Evergreen as a good fit because of my list, but I didn't *find it* because of my list.

Whether it's deciding where to live or what career you should pursue, it's important to make the best decision you can with the information you have today, and then to be willing and ready to adapt and change as you go into the future.

Opportunity

Where you decide to live will have a major impact on your life and the life of your future family. I recommend the following two steps to help guide you in making your decision.

First, use the list of questions that follow to help focus your search. Read through the list and then go back and mark them in order of importance to you. Place a #1 by the question that is most important, #2 by the second, and so on. After you've prioritized the questions go ahead and answer them.

How close will my immediate family be?

Where is the greatest opportunity to excel in my career?

Where do I want to raise my own family?

Will I have access to culture, art, and theater?

Will I have access to National Parks and nature?

Do I like the people I've met in the town? (Go to the grocery store to get a good idea about the locals.)

Where are the best schools?

Are there ways of entertaining guests and clients in the area?

Can I live with the climate and weather patterns?

Will I be able to pursue my favorite hobbies?

Where do I feel the safest?

Which town has the cleanest environment—air, water, and so on?

Is it a settled community or just a bedroom community?

Are there places to work out and exercise nearby?

Are there sidewalks for my children?

How close is the nearest major airport?

Where do I see myself wanting to live in 20 years?

Now that you have a clearer sense of what you want, the second step is, as Oriah said, to let go of any expectation of how it should be. Your list serves almost as a radio signal that broadcasts what you are looking for out into the universe. Once you make that broadcast, you need to wait patiently for the universe to present it or a better option to you. Easier said than done, but this is where the magic occurs. When you're open to the possibilities that will arise in your life, you'll be guided to that perfect place to live. Try it. You have nothing to lose and everything to gain.

alexis clements, 22

hometown:
kansas city, ks

favorite food:
thai

biggest concern:
finding the resources to pursue what makes me happy

last read: life after god by douglas coupland

best date advice: don't hold expectations

secret to life: following through

final thought: stop watching the news

CHAPTER TWENTY-NINE

What is my spiritual path?

Astronaut Edgar Mitchell remembers the exact moment his life changed. A graduate of a Massachusetts Institute of Technology doctorate program, Edgar was among the Apollo 14 crew that successfully landed on the moon in 1971. It was during the return trip to earth that his life was forever altered.

"A wonderful quietness had drifted into the cabin," Mitchell explains in his book *The Way of the Explorer*. "The sensation was altogether foreign. Somehow I felt tuned into something much larger than myself, something much larger than the planet in the window; something incomprehensibly big. Even today, the perceptions still baffle me."

Since that experience over 33 years ago, Mitchell has dedicated his life to researching human consciousness. In that single moment, he set foot on his spiritual path. He redirected his focus into an arena previously unknown to him: an exploration of the meaning and purpose of his life.

Mitchell is not alone. Many astronauts have reported similar "spiritual experiences" during space missions that changed their outlooks on life. For most of us, however, it's not a trip to the moon that prompts our spiritual journey, rather it's a feeling we get when we're watching the sunset over Lake Michigan, witnessing an eagle soaring in Alaska, walking the quiet streets of New York in the pre-dawn, holding the delicate body of a newborn, standing alone at the grave of a friend, gazing into the glow of a campfire, or looking into the eyes of a lover. It's in such moments as these that we, like Mitchell, get a glimpse

maguel hudson, 29

favorite food:
gumbo

biggest concern:
will i be
successful?

favorite movie:
five heart beats

best date advice:
be yourself

secret to life:
trust in god

of something incomprehensibly big. These instances are the seed crystals that prompt us to begin moving along our spiritual path. As spiritual teacher and author Wayne Dyer says, "We begin to realize we are spiritual beings having a human experience."

Your spiritual path is an individual path. Although it may involve a church, religion, or study group, it's really about experiencing a connection to yourself, others, the universe, and God. "I think there is a huge dichotomy between religion and spirituality," Nathan, my younger brother and a 25-year-old medical student, told me. "Religion is for the masses and spirituality is for the individual. For example, I personally grew up in religion—going to church every Sunday, confirmation classes, and Sunday school. I didn't really have to search it out for myself, and sometimes when things are handed to you, you just don't appreciate them or you don't understand them."

Nathan continued, "When I was in college, I eventually got the feeling for what spirituality meant. It's much more individualistic. It's something that's self-directed. I discovered I could go and explore the areas I was interested in and the things in which I believe. Rather than have dogma pushed upon me and holding me accountable, it was more of an enlightened experience to go and actively seek out spirituality; and it was much more positive than the gloom and doom of a lot of traditional religions."

Nathan, like other quarterlifers I have interviewed, adopted his spiritual path because he wanted something more out of life. He was successful in academics, athletics, and had many friends, yet he sensed life contained greater riches. This is the same thing that happened to actor/director Mel Gibson. During an interview he told Diane Sawyer, "Let's face it. I've been to the pinnacle of what secular utopia has to offer. I've got money, fame, this, that, and the other. It didn't matter. There wasn't enough. It's not good enough. It leaves you empty. The more you eat, the emptier you get. I think everybody gets to a point in

their life where that happens. They get to a moment of truth and go, 'Well, what's it all about?' "

When you get to that point, like Mitchell, Nathan, and Gibson, you demand a deeper experience in your life. This is the time that you may begin a Bikram yoga class, join a Bible study group, attend an Omega Institute conference, learn Transcendental Meditation, or stop eating pork! Why would you do any of these activities? They are methods that you hope will peel back the mundane-ness of everyday life and give you a glimpse into something much greater underlying it all. The ultimate goal of these activities is to heighten your awareness so that you may experience being fully alive. Unfortunately, this aspiration is often replaced by the idea that if a little of an activity is good, a lot is better.

"I think that people often make a mistake, when they start with spirituality, by trying to bite off too much," Joan Borysenko, former director of the Harvard Mind/Body Research clinic and author of *Mending the Body, Minding*

jenny fellner, 24

hometown:
sturgis, sd

last year:
starred in mamma
mia on broadway

biggest concern:
that i'll never
work again

favorite food:
peanut butter

**favorite place to
visit:** home

favorite movie:
harold and maude

secret to life:
honesty

read more of
what jenny had to
share in "what is
my purpose?"

the Mind, told me. "They say to themselves, 'Gee, I could go to that qigong class, I could go to that yoga class, I could learn to chant, I could meditate, I could juice, I'd better get up at three in the morning and do five hours a day.' Most human beings won't sustain that, and what I've seen people do is get into an all-or-nothing mode.

"What I say is start simple," Borysenko continued. "'Do what you can, not what you won't.' That's my motto. Five minutes of meditation a day will make a big difference. If you can commit to five minutes that's great. That's much better than committing to an hour that you don't get to."

Just like exercising a muscle or taking a shower, doing a moderate amount *every* day is more beneficial than doing a lot at once. Think about it! If you showered for five hours straight once a month, would that be as effective as showering ten minutes every day of the month? Would working out for a solid day and a half, four times a year be better than working out three times a week every week? Of course not! It is better to wash and work out regularly. The same goes for spirituality. Meditating five minutes a day cleans your mind just like daily showers clean your body. The key to discovering your spiritual path is to allow your spiritual practice to become a way of life.

When I was 20, I packed up a van and moved to northern California to live and work at an ashram. I had no idea what I was getting into. All I knew was that I needed to do it. My friends and family back home were terrified, and I could understand their concern. At the time, headlines across the country reported the group suicide of members of Heaven's Gate, a cult also located in California. They feared I was going to be brainwashed and end up with the same fate. But, just like there are good cups and bad cups of coffee, so it is with organizations. Fortunately, the ashram I moved to was a good one. Over the course of the four months that I lived there, I learned the tools of meditation, yoga, Ayurvedic health care, visualization, energizing exercises, vegetarian cooking, journaling, introspection, and daily study. Despite all these valuable tools, the greatest lesson I learned was from the people I met.

The ashram was part of a greater community that was established in the 1960s. It's one of the few successful communal living experiments surviving from that era. The doctors, artists, mothers, fathers, chefs, carpenters, therapists, authors, accountants, computer programmers, families, and gardeners who came to live in the community did so for one reason: to live their spiritual path.

For the first time, I experienced a group of people who came together in Sunday service, evening meditation, morning yoga, and even some meals for the sole purpose of devotion to God. But even more powerful to me than the scheduled meetings and events was the presence that members of the community exemplified. When I would help Graciela, the chef, in the kitchen it was the intention behind her work that inspired me. On the outside she was cooking, like any cook, and on the inside she was blessing the food, asking that

jay foss, 27

biggest concern: losing my personal freeedooom!!! on october 8th, 1998 jay's wife, erin, was diagnosed with a rare malignant brain tumor.

Jay's Journey: it's been an honor to be erin's caregiver. i suddenly was putting all of my energy and ability toward her care. if she was given a fifty percent chance of survival, my job was to make it sixty!

life motto: whatever it takes!

it infuse vitality and clarity into all who ate it.

Each morning, working with Graciela, we meditated and prayed before starting in the kitchen. While preparing food we chanted songs, talked about spiritual lessons, and listened to inspirational tapes. After the food was cooked, we carefully placed it in dishes, blessed it, and served it to others. There was no separation between work and spirituality. They were one. I learned that life doesn't have to be compartmentalized. I could integrate my spiritual life into my work, family, hobbies, and workouts through the intention behind those activities.

When the intention or purpose behind an activity is to experience a greater connection to yourself, others, the universe, and God, that activity becomes part of your spiritual path. This happened to Mitchell after his Apollo 14 mission. He combined his scientific knowledge and his newfound purpose of exploring human consciousness, and established the Institute of the Noetic Sciences. Gibson did the same thing when he combined his intention with his

Hollywood expertise and embarked on producing and directing the film *The Passion of the Christ*. He has said that making the film was "the most meaningful experience" of his life.

Opportunity

Your spiritual path is an individual journey to experience new depths of connection to yourself, others, the universe, and God. The first step in discovering your spiritual path is *not* to separate spirituality from the rest of your life. Instead infuse spirituality into your work, family, hobbies, sports, and daily activities through your intention. When your intention is to experience a connection to God's great creation, you can be shopping at the grocery store, stopped at a red light, sitting in church, standing on a mountaintop, or strolling with your kids through a museum and you will discover ways to make life a spiritual practice.

A simple way to establish your intention is to develop a habit of pausing before you embark on any activity. Taking a brief moment to focus your awareness makes all

more from jay...

most profound lesson: the realization that there is serious pain and sorrow in our midst. what's more, i realized that i have something significant to offer those afflicted. my eyes were opened to a universe of compassion and courage that i was not aware existed.

how is erin: today erin is the longest known survivor worldwide with her particular cancer. her outlook continues to be very good.

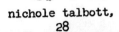

**nichole talbott,
28**

favorite movie:
princess bride

best date advice:
just be yourself

**worst date
advice:** no
kissing on the
first date

favorite book:
the giving tree

**what you wish
you knew two
years ago:** that
everything will
work itself out

life motto: take
advantage of
opportunities

the difference in daily living. A statement I have found valuable when I need to re-focus my intention is *How can I share love in this moment?* By simply pausing and saying that to myself before entering into a conversation, task, or project, I have found that events flow more smoothly and I feel a deeper connection to my life. This is the same concept behind the popular "WWJD" bracelets. For Christians who have a personal relationship with Jesus Christ, reflecting on the question, "What would Jesus do?" is a way of asking that their thoughts and actions be guided by love.

For the next week, try nothing more than to remind yourself: *How can I share love in this moment?* It may be helpful to write it on post-it notes and place them on your steering wheel and computer monitor, next to your toothbrush, and any other spot where you are likely to see them. This is a powerful reminder that every interaction and activity is an opportunity for spiritual growth.

CHAPTER THIRTY

How can I make my "mark" in this world?

"Can you help me get it off?" Luke Tresoglavic, 22, of Australia, yelled up to the lifeguard. He had been snorkeling off a coral reef when a two-foot long carpet shark bit into his leg and refused to let go.

"I just realized I had to swim in like that, hanging on to it," Luke later said, after swimming over 100 yards. "Once I got to shore, a couple of people tried to help me, but I could not remove it. It was stuck there, so I got up into my car and then drove to the clubhouse, and luckily the guys down there had a clue what to do."

Seeing Luke hobble into the clubhouse, several astounded lifeguards rushed to pry the shark from his leg. Once his leg was free, Luke was fine except for 70 needle-like punctures that were oozing with blood.

Certainly the shark left its mark. What will be yours? Everybody wants to leave a mark in this world. We want to make a difference—to be remembered.

This motivation is what prompted Mark Carmichael to begin painting a baseball 27 years ago. Nearly every day he walks back to his shed where the ball is suspended and paints on a fresh layer. Now, with over 18,000 layers of paint covering it, the ball weighs 1,300 pounds. It will go into the Guinness Book of Records as the world's largest painted ball.

Why did Mark spend a quarter of a century painting a baseball? Why do people write books, raise children, volunteer, and develop

will logsdon, 16

favorite food:
pizza with ranch
dressing

biggest concern:
the real world

favorite movie:
tin cup

best date advice:
be yourself

favorite book:
my side of the
mountain

**what you wish you
knew two years
ago:** i wish i
would have
known...?

life motto:
"celebrate we
will, because
life is short
but sweet for
certain"-dave
matthews band

businesses? Often we do these activities because we want to leave a legacy. We want something we said, did, or created to continue to have an impact after we are dead and gone. It has been said that we spend the first half of our lives establishing our legitimacy—trying to prove ourselves—and the second half building a legacy. But today's quarterlifers aren't waiting. We are looking for ways to establish our legacy today.

When Jason Regier was just 21 years old he was driving from Denver, Colorado back to Oregon State University for his final semester of college. Heading out of Salt Lake City, Utah on I-80, Jason did what we've all done. He looked down and began flipping through stations on his radio. As he searched the airwaves his Jeep Cherokee drifted off of the interstate onto the road's steep shoulder. Startled Jason jerked the SUV back onto I-80, but the front tires caught causing his vehicle to roll and roll and roll. Two days later Jason woke up in Craig Hospital paralyzed from the neck down. A division I soccer player and just four months away from graduating, he now had to learn how to brush his teeth again.

I met and interviewed Jason eight years after his accident. Now 29, in a wheelchair and permanently paralyzed from the chest down, he has finished his undergraduate degree, worked as a corporate trainer, coached a soccer team, spoken to entire high school and college classes, and most recently went back and earned a masters in business.

Jason was an unusual guest for the tv show. Up until his interview, every person I'd invited on had either written a book, traveled the country speaking, or had some form of expertise. Jason was just an ordinary guy who had been placed in extraordinary circumstances. But despite not having an "expertise" I still asked Jason big, challenging questions. Did he think life was fair? Had he ever considered suicide? What was the meaning of life? For every question I asked Jason, he had an answer that was raw, profound, and not some sound bite he had said

hundreds of other times. Instead he spoke from the depth of his being.

In the "Introduction" I told you that I've interviewed over 300 quarterlifers for this book and that I'd come to realize that our generation knows far more than we give ourselves credit for. All that began with Jason's interview. He was quarterlife interview number one and left such a mark it prompted me to wonder, "Do other quarterlifers have just as much to share if given the chance?"

At the end of Jason's interview, I asked him how each of us in our generation—who are surrounded by mega successful peers like musicians Jewel, John Mayer, and Usher; athletes like Carmelo Anthony, Venus Williams, and Tiger Woods; actors like Jennifer Garner and Leonardo DiCaprio; and directors like Zack Braff——can make our mark in this world just as he had made a mark on my life and the lives of all the audiences he addresses?

"Before the accident there were 10,000 things I could do with my life. I had everything going for me,"

sierra trujillo, 24

occupation:
student and office manager

favorite song:
crush by dave matthews band

favorite food:
sushi

biggest concern:
financial independence—i want to be able to support myself and not have to constantly worry about money

date advice:
be yourself. if the person doesn't like who you are, change isn't worth the headache.

Jason told me. "Now, realistically, there are maybe a 100 things I can do. But the fact of the matter is that most of us only ever get around to really doing about 40 things in our life. So although I can't do as many I can still do just as much. The key for me as it is for anyone is to get started. To get started today living the life I want to live."

Jason went on to say, "That's the beauty of this world. Change is very rarely made in big bangs. Making a mark is really about making a contribution. It doesn't happen overnight. I've been working at getting my life back twenty-four hours a day, seven days a week. You find small little things and start.

"We need to ask ourselves, 'What can I do today to make the world a better place?' That is the mark each of us will leave in history. Who comes after us will be living with the choices we make. That's the legacy of who we are."

Jason is not alone. Time and time again I have heard from guests on my TV and radio shows that the secret is not in focusing on making your mark, rather it is focusing on making a contribution. As peace activist Coleman McCarthy said, "Few of us will ever be called on to do great things, but all of us can do small things in a great way."

Growing up in the Black Hills of South Dakota, I immersed myself in the culture and traditions of the Lakota Sioux. On several occasions I fasted overnight on Bear Butte and Harney Peak, two very sacred peaks to the Lakota tribe. During one outing, I met a man who taught me about the concept of the Seventh Generation. It's a Native American practice of asking *How will this impact the seventh generation of people who come after me?* before one takes action. Can you imagine how different our world would be today if everyone looked at the short- *and* long-term impact of their daily thoughts, choices, and actions?

The fact of the matter is that society rarely pays attention to the ultimate impact of our current actions. It is precisely because of this lack of future vision that our parents' and grandparents' generations have vastly destroyed our forests,

polluted our air and water, exploited our natural resources, overspent our budget, and—recently—created ill will with the governments of foreign nations around the world. Now it is our turn to do something about it. If we continue to do what has been done we will pollute, over-populate, alienate, and over-consume ourselves right into extinction.

It's not a question of whether or not you can make a mark in this world. Anyone can. It's a question of what kind of mark you make.

I'd be willing to bet that I had one of the most scenic drives to high school in the United States. The road known as "the S curves" weaves through a canyon of towering sandstone cliffs alongside a winding stream. The natural beauty of this area would attract hikers, photographers, bikers, and fly fisherman except that it is being destroyed. Starting the year before I graduated, seniors spray painted "93 rules" on the virgin sandstone cliffs. Now each year for over a decade members of the graduating class have been scarring the natural

john formento, 28

hometown:
philadelphia, pa

favorite movie:
scarface

biggest concern:
employment—will
i be able to use
the degree i just
spent all that
money to acquire?

life motto: live
each day to the
fullest

a special thanks
to john for
taking many of
the pictures in
this book.

beauty of the rock walls with their own class numbers.

Unfortunately, it is not easy to restore the cliff once the paint damage has been done. The same goes for damage to relationships with friends, family, other nations, and the environment. This is why our generation must demand a level of awareness never seen before. We must understand that the marks we are making today can build or break the human race and the planet. The good news is that our generation is making a shift. Quarterlifers from all walks of life have shared with me their desire to leave the earth a better place.

As Vivian, 24, a music and biology student in Miami, Florida told me, "To me, it doesn't have to be that I'm on every magazine. My mark in this world is making a difference in somebody's life. With music, I want to touch the children who would not have had the opportunity to play an instrument or be exposed to the world of music. I was given that same opportunity when I was younger. It doesn't matter how big or small, I just want to touch somebody's life."

Like Vivian and Jason, each of us can make our mark and leave this world a better place. We accomplish this the moment we look beyond our immediate short-term benefit and ask what impact will this have on ourselves, others, and the Earth in the future.

Opportunity

The secret to making a lasting mark is your awareness. When you're living consciously, every thought and action goes toward creating a beneficial impact in the world. Nathaniel Branden, former associate with Ayn Rand and author of *The Art of Living Consciously*, told me, "Living consciously means being present to what you're doing while you're doing it."

To stay conscious on a daily basis, I recommend a sentence completion tool that Branden taught me. The process is straightforward. Each day, place the following sentence stems in front of you:

If I bring 5 percent more awareness to the legacy I want to leave, then—.

---

more from John...

difference between our generation and our parents: things are more laid back today than they were for our parents. for example, men don't think women want to be treated like a lady, but they do.

what you wish you knew two years ago: i wish that i would have taken school a little more seriously. i did a lot of screwing around, and now i want to get my life going, but feel a little off.

read more of what John had to share in "how do i make these major life decisions?"

brittanie rockhill, 19

occupation:
student

biggest concern:
making choices
now that will
not guide my life
in the direction
i aspire to
go; dating the
wrong people;
and studying
irrelevant
material

favorite food:
mango

**worst date
advice:** thinking
that spending a
short amount of
time with someone
has entitled
you to actually
knowing them

secret to life:
balance

*If I bring 5 percent more awareness
to the long-term impact of my daily
thoughts, choices, and actions,
then—.*

Take a few minutes to write down ten completed sentences for each of the stems above. For example: If I bring 5 percent more awareness to the legacy I want to leave, then I spend less time watching television and more time writing my book. What will happen over the course of a week is that you flood your awareness with what you can do to make your mark in the world. These exercises keep your awareness levels from drifting off. As Branden says, "I use sentence completions to stimulate raising the level of consciousness."

After a week, take a close look at your lists and then ask the following question: *I am becoming aware that . . . ?* What you will discover is that certain activities continually show up on your list. These activities can then become your starting point. Use them to start taking action to make your mark in the world.

Summary

Each of us knows far more than we give ourselves credit for. As quarterlifers our major hurdle is that we have not yet learned to trust ourselves or the process of making our way into the real world.

Often we read a book, hear a speaker, or watch a talk show and think, "Wow, that's brilliant. She is really talking to me." The only reason the "expert's" words resonate with us is because he or she has given voice to what we already know to be true, but have never had a platform to express it through.

Think about it. When was the last time someone asked you the following questions: "What is the meaning of life?" "How do you discover your purpose?" and "What is your spiritual path?" I bet you've never been asked all those questions. Neither had the 300 quarterlifers I interviewed, yet every one of them

had something profound to share when given the chance.

T.S. Eliot, the poet, once wrote:

And the end of all our exploring
Will be to arrive where we started
And know the place for the first
time.

Eliot points out, the journey of life is to go full circle, coming back to where you first began, and knowing it truly for the first time. Think about how much more relaxed and confident you are about a situation, like buying a computer, if you've done it before. The pitfall is that as quarterlifers most things we haven't done before. As a result we end up stressing and worrying for years only to look back from the vantage point of the future and say, "Oh, it really wasn't that bad. I wasted a lot of worrying."

Why wait for the vantage point of 20/20 hindsight to realize you're going to be just fine? Ultimately you're either going to survive or die. If you're dead you have nothing to worry about so why not allow yourself to enjoy life the first time through?

It's possible to enjoy life as a quarterlifer when you realize you're being provided all the tools you need to take your next step forward. When you truly understand that Somebody out there is plotting to do you good, that is the moment the confusion, frustration, and desperation turns into certainty, joy, and confidence.

Each "Opportunity" section of this book provides techniques that you can use to better see the direction and purpose in your life and relationships. Perhaps the greatest technique is to simply begin asking yourself and others the big questions of life. Give yourself a chance to respond. You'll be surprised at what you have to say.

As I said in the "Introduction" I say again now. Thank you for joining me on this journey. May this book change your life for the better as much as the writing of it has changed mine. This truly is the book that I wish I'd had when I was entering the real world. I look forward to the day when we meet in person.

Jason Steinle

Evergreen, Colorado

The experts

WHERE IN THE BOOK TO FIND THE EXPERTS WHO WERE INTERVIEWED

Gary Zukav After Oprah discovered Zukav's book *The Seat of the Soul* he became a regular on *The Oprah Winfrey Show*. He and his partner Linda Francis co-founded the non-profit Seat of the Soul Foundation and together wrote *The Heart of the Soul* and *The Mind of the Soul*. Look for what Zukav shared in "How Can I Overcome This Empty Pit Feeling Inside?" **www.zukav.com**

Zig Ziglar Since 1970, Ziglar has traveled over five million miles around the world inspiring and transforming audiences. He has shared the platform with Dr. Norman Vincent Peale, President Reagan, and Dr. Robert Schuller. Ziglar is the author of the book

See You at the Top and *Success for Dummies*. Look for what Ziglar shared in "What Is the Key to a Successful Marriage?" **www.ziglar.com**

Abby Wilner Seeing similar uncertainty in her and her friends' lives, Wilner teamed up with Alexandra Robbins and coined the phrase "quarterlife crisis." Together they wrote the best-seller *Quarterlife Crisis*. Look for what Wilner shared in "What is the Real World?" **www.quarterlifecrisis.com**

Marianne Williamson Since 1983, Williamson has lectured professionally around the world. She co-founded the Global Renaissance Alliance, a worldwide network of peace activists and is the author of the *New York Times* #1 best selling books *A Return to Love* and *Everyday Grace*. Look for what Williamson shared in "When Should I Marry?" **www.mariannewilliamson.com**

Erik Weihenmayer On May 25, 2001, Weihenmayer became the first blind climber in history to reach the summit of the world's highest mountain, Mt. Everest. He is the author of *Touch the Top of the World*. Look for what Weihenmayer shared in "Is Life Fair?" **www.touchthetop.com**

Ethan Watters On a personal quest to find out why he was still single well into his 30s, Watters realized that he only had to look as far as his own social circle to see that he is not alone. He is the author of the book *Urban Tribes*, a book about the communities of young people across the country who live, work, and play together in various combinations. Look for what Watter shared in "When Should I Have Children?" **www.urbantribes.net**

Larry Voorhees A former high school shop teacher, Voorhees began studying the principles of financial literacy over 25 years ago. He then left teaching and became a consultant with Primerica Financial Group. Today he is financially independent. Look for what Voorhees shared in "Where Should I Invest My Money?" **www.primerica.com**

Brian Tracy Each year Tracy speaks to more than 250,000 men and women. His book, *Success is a Journey*, which tells of a great adventure he had as a quarterlifer, is one of my favorites. In addition he is the most listened to audiotape author on personal and business success in the world. Look for what Tracy shared in "How can I Stay Motivated?" **www.briantracy.com**

Chuck Sorenson A Methodist minister, psychologist, and long time consultant to dentists, chiropractors, and medical doctors, Sorenson has personally had a significant impact on both my personal and professional life. Look for what Sorenson shared in "When Should I Marry?" **www.bullcrane.com/cmsassoc/**

Lance Smith Once told by a teacher that he should learn sign language because he had delayed speech development, today Smith presents his message of hope and integrity throughout school systems. He is the author of the book *My Name is Victory*. Look for what Smith shared in "How Can I Make Money?" **www.claysmile.com**

Brigitte Secard Tired of spiritual co-dependency, Secard renounced gurus and sought out self-truth instead of self-help. She is the author of the book *Soulfire*. Look for what Secard shared in "Am I with the Right One?" **www.selftruth.com**

Cynthia Ryk A consultant in the areas of leadership and career development, Ryk has been working with corporations and individuals since 1986. She is the founder of the Art of Living Truth. Look for what Ryk shared in "What Should I Do for a Living?" **www.cynthiaryk.com**

Jay Edward Russo A professor of Marketing and Behavior Science at Cornell University, Russo's research centers on decision-making for managers and consumers. He is the co-author of the book *Winning Decisions*. Look for what Russo shared in "How Do I Make These Major Life Decisions?"

Maria Nemeth A clinical psychologist with more than 28 years of experience and a former professor at the University of California-Davis School of Medicine, Nemeth is the author of *The Energy of Money*. Look for what Nemeth shared in "How Can I Make Money?" **www.marianemeth.com**

Margret McBride Within one year of starting her literary agency in 1980, McBride successfully sold the national bestseller *The One Minute Manager*. Over 20 years later she teamed up with **Ken Blanchard**, the co-author of *The One Minute Manager*, and wrote *The One Minute Apology*. Look for what McBride shared in "What Is the Meaning of Life?" **www.mcbrideliterary.com**

Mary LoVerde Former Director of the Hypertension Research Center at the University of Colorado

School of Medicine, LoVerde is the author of *Stop Screaming at the Microwave* and *I Used to Have a Handle on Life but It Broke*. Look for what LoVerde shared in "What Can I Do About All This Stress?" **www.maryloverde.com**

Ted Kerasote A regular writer for periodicals, including *Outside* and *National Geographic Traveler*, Keresote wrote the book *Out There in the Wild in a Wired Age* following a canoe trip along one of the most remote rivers in the world. Look for what Keresote shared in "Should I Travel and Explore Before Settling Down?"

Willie Jolley Voted one of the outstanding five speakers in the world by Toastmasters International, Jolley is the author of *A Setback Is a Setup for a Comeback* and *It Only Takes a Moment to Change Your Life*. Look for what Jolley shared in "How Can I Overcome My Fear of Failure?" **www.williejolley.com**

Marilyn Innerfeld Through her diagnosis and eventual survival of cancer, Innerfeld wrote *Healing Through Love* and co-founded The Worldwide Center. Look for what Innerfeld shared in "When Is It Time to End a Relationship?" **www.expandedliving.net**

Nancy Cook De Herrera A fascinating woman whose friendship with the founding father of Transcendental Mediation, Maharishi Mahesh Yogi, led her to spend time in India with the Beatles, Mia Farrow, Mike Love, and Donovan. She writes about India and her life in *All You Need Is Love*. Look for what Herrera shared in "Does Anyone Have It All Figured Out?"

Gay and Kathlyn Hendricks Married for over 24 years, the Hendricks travel the world sharing the keys to a lasting and loving relationship. They are the authors of *Conscious Living* and *Conscious Loving*. Look for what the Hendricks shared in "Can I Be in a Relationship and Still Be Successful?" **www.hendricks.com**

Mark Victor Hansen For 25 years, Hansen has focused

on helping individuals and organizations awaken possibilities. He is the co-author of *The One Minute Millionaire* and best-selling *Chicken Soup for the Soul* series. Look for what Hansen shared in "What Is My Purpose?"
www.markvictorhansen.com

Marlys Hanson An insightful woman who has nearly three decades of experience as a consultant on career choices. Her book *Passion and Purpose* had a significant impact on my life. Look for what Hanson shared in "What Is My Purpose?"
www.motivationalpattern.com

Stephanie Gunning Former senior editor at Bantam Doubleday Dell, Gunning ventured out and began her own editing company. Not only is she directly quoted, her influence is felt on each page. This book would not be in your hands right now had it not been for Gunning's guidance and encouragement. Look for what Gunning shared in "What Is the Real World?"
www.stephaniegunning.com

John Gray Gray is the author of 15 best-selling books, including *Men Are from Mars, Women Are from Venus*, the number one best-selling book of the last decade. Over 30 million Mars and Venus books have been sold in over 40 languages throughout the world. Look for what Gray shared in "Where Can I Find Mr. or Ms. Right?"
www.marsvenus.com

Patrick Gentempo A leader in the wellness and chiropractic fields, Gentempo is the co-founder of the Chiropractic Leadership Alliance and the Creating Wellness Alliance. Look for what Gentempo shared in "Is a Life of Purpose Easy?"
www.subluxation.com

Debbie Ford For ten years Debbie has been lecturing and leading workshops around the country, bringing to life the processes from her books *The Right Questions* and *The Dark Side of the Light Chasers*. Look for what Ford shared in "How Do I Make These Major Life Decisions?"
www.debbieford.com

Jason Dorsey To publish his first book, *Graduate to Your Perfect Job*, Dorsey accumulated over $50,000 in debt before age 19. Since that first book he has traveled the world speaking to quarterlifers. Last year alone he spoke to over 100,000 people. Look for what Dorsey shared in "Is Life Fair?" **www.jasondorsey.com**

Oriah Mountain Dreamer Unknown to her, Oriah's poem *The Invitation* was placed on the internet. Within a year, taking on a life of its own, the poem spread around the world deeply touching the lives of those who read it. From this original poem, Oriah went on to author three bestselling books: *The Invitation*, *The Dance*, and *The Call*. Look for what Oriah shared in "Where Should I Live?" **www.oriah mountaindreamer.com**

John Demartini One of the great teachers early in my personal and professional life, Demartini is the author of *Count Your Blessings* and *The Breakthrough Experience*. Look for what Demartini shared

in "How Can I Stay Motivated?" **www.drdemartini.com**

Charlie Daniels A legendary country/rock singer, Daniels is just as pleasant to talk to as he is talented. Although he's best known for hits like "The Devil Went Down to Georgia," Daniels is also the author of *Ain't No Rag*. Look for what Daniels shared in "What Should I Do for a Living?" **www.charliedanielsband.com**

Sean Covey Former starting quarterback at Brigham Young University, Covey earned his MBA from Harvard Business School and went on to write *The 7 Habits of Highly Effective Teenagers*, a spin-off of his father's classic book, *The 7 Habits of Highly Effective People*. Look for what Covey shared in "Is a Life of Purpose Easy?" **www.franklincovey.com**

Robert K. Cooper Named "the ultimate business guru for the new millennium" by *USA Today*, Cooper is the author of *The Other 90%*, *The Performance Edge*, and *Excelerating*. Look for what

Cooper shared in "Who Am I?" **www.robertkcooper.com**

Jack Canfield Considered one of the world's leading authorities on self-esteem, Canfield is a graduate of Harvard and co-author of the *Chicken Soup for the Soul* series. His personal example, books, and audio programs have been very influential in my life, and in the creation of this book. Look for what Canfield shared in "How Can I Stay Motivated?" **www.jackcanfield.com**

Sasha Cagen Cagen coined the phrase "quirkyalone," which started as an article in the *Utne* and grew into an international conversation. She is the author of the book *Quirkyalone*. Look for what Cagen shared in "Am I with the Right One?" **www.quirkyalone.net**

Po Bronson Questioning in his own life what he should do for a living, Bronson began traveling around the United States asking others how they had answered that very question. Over 900 interviews later, Bronson shares what he learned in his bestseller

What Should I Do with My Life? Look for what Bronson shared in "Should I Go for the Big Bucks or Pursue What I Truly Want to Do?" **www.pobronson.com**

Ed Brodow A former marine, Brodow pursued his interest in acting and landed leads in several American and European feature films. Drawing from his stage experience, Brodow now travels the country teaching audiences the art of negotiation. He is the author of *Beating the Success Trap*. Look for what Brodow shares in "What Is the Meaning of Life?" **www.brodow.com**

Nathaniel Branden A pioneer and leader in the field of self-esteem, Branden has done more, perhaps, than any other theorist to awaken America's consciousness to the importance of self-esteem. His book *The Art of Living Consciously* is a must-read for anyone looking to take responsibility for his or her life. Look for what Branden shared in "How Can I Make My 'Mark' in This World?" **www.nathanielbranden.com**

Joan Borysenko Former Harvard medical scientist and psychologist, Borysenko co-founded the Mind-Body clinical programs at two Harvard Medical School teaching hospitals. She is the author of the bestseller *Minding the Body, Mending the Mind* and *Inner Peace for Busy People*. Look for what Borysenko shared in "What Is My Spiritual Path?" **www.joanborysenko.com**

Paul Argentiere Saving his own relationship from disaster, Argentiere sat down and wrote out hundreds of pages of notes. After revising these notes several times he wrote *The Get-It-Together Process*, a concise and very practical book on reviving relationships. Look for what Argentiere shared in "What Is the Key to a Successful Marriage?" **www.get-it-together.com**

Mark Albion Former professor of marketing at Harvard Business School, Albion left Harvard and went on to write *Making a Life, Making a Living*. Look for what Albion shared in "Does Becoming a Responsible Adult Mean Life Becomes Boring and Monotonous?" **www.makingalife.com**

AUTHORS AND BOOKS]

Recommendations

FINDING YOUR PURPOSE

Mark Albion, author of
Making a Life, Making a Living,
www.makingalife.com

Ed Brodow, author of *Beating the
Success Trap*, www.brodow.com

Po Bronson, author of *What
Should I do for a Living?*,
www.pobronson.com

Oriah Mountain Dreamer, author
of *The Call*, www.oriahmountain
dreamer.com

Debbie Ford, author of *The Right
Questions*, www.debbieford.com

Marlys Hansen, author of *Passion
and Purpose*, www.motivational
pattern.com

Jean Houston, author of
A Passion for the Possible,
www.jeanhouston.org

Tama Kieves, author of *This Time
I Dance*, www.thistimeidance.com

Ian Percy, author of *The 7
Secrets to a Life of Meaning*,
www.ianpercy.com

Brigitte Secard, author of *Soulfire*,
www.selftruth.com

GETTING AHEAD

**Jack Canfield and Mark Victor
Hansen**, authors of *The Power of
Focus*, www.jackcanfield.com and
www.markvictorhansen.com

Sean Covey, author of *The 7
Habits of Highly Effective Teens*,
www.franklincovey.com

Steven Covey, author
of *First Things First*,
www.franklincovey.com

Robert K. Cooper,
author of *The Other 90%*,
www.robertkcooper.com

John Demartini, author of
The Breakthrough Experience,
www.drdemartini.com

Jean Houston, author of
A Passion for the Possible,
www.jeanhouston.org

Willie Jolley, author of *A
Setback Is a Setup for a Comeback,*
www.williejolley.com

Anthony Robbins, author
of *Unlimited Power,*
www.tonyrobbins.com

David Schwartz, author of *The
Magic of Thinking Big*

Marilyn Tam, author of *How to
Use What You've Got to Get What
You Want,* www.howtousewhat
youvegot.com

Brian Tracy, author of *Focal Point,*
www.briantracy.com

Zig Ziglar, author of *See You at the
Top,* www.ziglar.com

INSPIRATION

**Jack Canfield and Mark Victor
Hansen**, authors of the *Chicken
Soup for the Soul* series,
www.chickensoupforthesoul.com

Jeffrey Alan Hall, author
of *An Awakening Within,*
www.jeffreyalanhall.com

Erik Weihnmeyer, author
of *Touch the Top of the World,*
www.touchthetop.com

CONSCIOUS LIVING

Nathaniel Branden, author of
The Art of Living Consciously,
www.nathanielbranden.com

Joan Borysenko, author of
Inner Peace for Busy People,
www.joanborysenko.com

Ralph Waldo Emerson, author the
essays *Self-Reliance and Nature*

David R. Hawkins,
author of *Power vs. Force,*
www.powervsforce.com

Mary LoVerde, author of *Stop
Screaming at the Microwave,*
www.maryloverde.com

Ted Kerasote, author of *Out There
in the Wild in a Wired Age*

Don Miguel Ruiz, author of *The
Four Agreements*

Recommendations

Diane Sieg, author of *Stop Living Life like an Emergency*, www.dianesieg.com

Bernie Siegel, author of *How to Live Between Office Visits*

Gary Zukav, author of *The Mind of the Soul*, www.zukav.com

RELATIONSHIPS

Paul Argentiere, author of *The Get-It-Together Process*, www.get-it-together.com

Sasha Cagan, author of *Quirkyalone*, www.quirkyalone.net

Paul Ferrini, author of *Creating a Spiritual Relationship*

John Gray, author of *Men are from Mars, Women are from Venus*, www.marsvenus.com

Gay and Kathlyn Hendricks, authors of *Lasting Love*, www.hendricks.com

Gary Michael, author of *Across a Crowded Room*, www.drgarymichael.com

SPIRITUALITY

Deepak Chopra, author of *How to Know God*, www.chopra.com

Ram Dass, author of *Grist for the Mill*

Nancy Cooke de Herrera, author of *All you Need is Love*

Jean Houston, author of *The Search for the Beloved*, www.jeanhouston.org

Sharon Salzberg, author of *Faith*, www.sharonsalzberg.com

Wayne Dyer, author of *There's a Spiritual Solution to Every Problem*, www.drwaynedyer.com

Bruce Wilkinson, author of *The Prayer of Jabez*, www.prayerofjabez.com

Marianne Williamson, author of *A Return to Love*, www.marianne.com

MONEY

Robert Allen and Mark Victor Hansen, authors of the *One Minute Millionaire*, www.oneminute millionaire.com

John Demartini, author of *The Secrets to Financial Mastery*, **www.drdemartini.com**

Napolean Hill, author of *Think and Grow Rich*

George S. Clason, author of *The Richest Man in Babylon*

William J. O'Neil, author of *The 24 Essential Lessons for Investment Success*

Robert T. Kiyosaki, author of *Rich Dad, Poor Dad*, **www.richdad.com**

Suze Orman, author of *9 Steps to Financial Freedom*, **www.suzeorman.com**

Thomas Stanley and William Danko, authors of *The Millionaire Next Door*

Lynne Twist, author of *The Soul of Money*, **www.soulofmoney.org**

Ethan Watters, author of *Urban Tribes*, **www.urbantribes.net**

Abby Wilner and Alexandra Robbins, authors of *Quarterlife Crisis*, **www.quarterlifecrisis.com**

QUARTERLIFE MATERIALS

Jason Dorsey, author of *Graduate to your Perfect Job!*, **www.jasondorsey.com**

Lance Smith, author of *My Name is Victory*, **www.claysmile.com**

Acknowledgments

This book has been a dream three years in the making. So many people encouraged and guided me throughout the entire process. I want to acknowledge everyone who participated and thank each of you for your support.

To all the quarterlifers who openly shared their stories and understandings, your sincerity and frankness renewed my hope in our generation. Through our conversations I've deepened old friendships and forged new ones. For that I am grateful.

Thank you Greg Markle and Bob Bacon at KYGT 102.7FM for putting me on the air. It all started in the Goat Shack four years ago. Thank you Rasoj Shrestha and Stanley Li at Denver Community Television for providing me with a television show. Without all of you none of this would have been possible.

Thank you John Fortin for your expertise in the control and editing room. You took the television show from rough beginnings and made it great. We may have lost a few hairs, but it's been fun. Thank you Ace Miller for your creative input and editing skill. Bob Coberly and Fred Parker deserve a big thanks for running the cameras, setting up, and tearing down the set.

Thank you to all the authors, speakers, musicians, doctors, actors, and consultants who have shared their time and insights on *The Steinle Show* radio and television programs. Each of you has impacted my life and helped me move forward in this project. I met you all as experts and left knowing you as friends.

Stephanie Gunning, thank you for your editing wisdom. I thoroughly enjoyed our Friday morning conversations. Sara Dykstra, Susan

Brown, and Mom, thank you for your in-depth suggestions on the manuscript. John Formento, thank you for taking the photos throughout this book. Michele Renée Ledoux, thank you for taking the ideas and concepts I had for the book's design and making them concrete.

Thank you Sam Charchian and the rest of the Cosmpolitan Toastmasters. Your frank evaluations with sincere advice provided the perfect environment for me to speak out. Thank you Doctors Joseph Sweere, Kevin Kalb, Terry Erickson, and Noni Threinen for providing me opportunities to find my speaking rhythm.

Thank you Anandi Cornell, Diksha McCord, Gyandev McCord, Wayne Palmer, Graciela and all the guests I met during my time at the Expanding Light. The philosophy and practices I learned in those four-months permeate my life today.

Thank you Joel Roberts for your excellent media program which pointed me in the direction of this book. Your words of encouragement gave me the motivation to start this project over from scratch a year ago.

Thank you Mark Victor Hansen and Jack Canfield for providing me guidance in the all-too-new world of book publishing. Your examples and resources have been steady lighthouses on my journey.

To all the people at Health and Harmony, PC thank you for your support, interest, and input. Art and Ronnie Zeise, Marilyn McDermond, Barbara Stinson, Bonny and Bruce Hansen, Bernie Watts, Ben Carter, Dale Parker, Jeanne and Roger Ambrosier, and so, so many more (you all know who you are). You have all been like family.

Thank you community of Evergreen for introducing me to so many wonderful people. Chuck Sorenson, your consulting on this project and others has guided me to reprioritize my life. It's been wonderful working with you. Thank you Gabija McLauchlan for making me aware of the possibilities

Acknowledgments

in my personal and professional life. Thank you Chris Lenick for sharing with me your journey through the book publishing industry. Thank you Jeffrey Alan Hall for being the first guest ever on our radio show. Thank you Mary Jo Nelson and Carrie Kubesa at Mail Boxes Etc. for your help and for allowing me "behind the scenes access" to your computers and printers. Thank you to Evergreen Fitness Center for allowing me a wonderful place to workout and clear my mind as this book came together.

Thank you Mom and Dad. I dedicated this book to you because your support and love has moved me forward more than you may ever know. To my brothers, Nathan and Tyler, thanks for your love, guidance and input. I'm very proud of both of you.

Above all, thank you Lord for providing me this opportunity to share Your message of hope and love.

sharing a message of hope and love...

About the author

Jason Steinle is host of *The Steinle Show* radio and television talk show programs featuring interviews with the world's top experts in career development, relationships, spirituality, health, and business. In addition, Jason is the founder of Health and Harmony, PC, a chiropractic and wellness center in Evergreen, Colorado. He completed his Bachelor of Human Biology and Doctor of Chiropractic degrees at Northwestern Chiropractic College in Minneapolis, MN.

Being a quarterlifer himself, Jason Steinle knows firsthand the questions, concerns, and problems his peers face. By virtue of his research and talk show interviews, Jason's writings contain the essence of hundreds of years of experts' wisdom and experience applied to the current concerns of today's quarterlifers. Jason has also gleaned

years of experience and insight from the patients he works with on a daily basis at Health and Harmony, PC, a center he founded at age 24. He has heard thousands of stories and lessons from these real people seeking to live purpose-filled lives.

One of Jason's great loves is public speaking. His experience as a public speaker includes being awarded the Competent Toastmasters Award from Toastmaster's International. He has spoken at Colorado State University, Black Hills State University, Northwestern Health Science University, and to many community groups in Colorado and Minnesota.

Beyond his professional work, what Jason is most thankful for are the people in his life. Blessed with wonderful parents and two younger brothers, his family has been a backbone of support in his life. Since moving to Evergreen, Colorado, Jason has adopted a much larger family. Through his work at Health and Harmony, PC, patients that entered his life as clients remain as cherished lifelong friends.

QUARTERLIFE SOLUTIONS]

Programs

Bring the UPLOAD EXPERIENCE
to your college campus or organization
with:

QUARTERLIFE SOLUTIONS *live*

"*Upload a Lifetime of Experience
in a Single Seminar!*"

Bring the core of this book and
Jason's research to your own town,
school, and club.

Please visit the
Upload Experience website

www.UploadExperience.com

for more information on
specific programs.

"Jason Steinle is one of the great
young speakers of our time! Jason
expertly combines the knowledge
he has gleaned from interviewing
the world's top experts with the
vantage point of someone still in
his twenties. I highly recommend
his presentations for 20- and 30-
year-olds today!"

—**Ed Tate**, Winner of the
Toastmasters' International 2000
World Championship of Public
Speaking

MORE PRAISE FOR UPLOAD EXPERIENCE LIVE PROGRAMS

"Self-esteem, while barely touched upon in the educational system, is critical for the success of today's college graduate. Jason Steinle's program fills this void. He has researched the questions young people face when leaving college and put together a powerful program that addresses these concerns. I recommend him as a critical part of your student's education!"

—Nathaniel Branden, PhD, author of *The Art of Living Consciously* and *The Six Pillars of Self-Esteem*

"Success in life, whether it's reaching the summit of Mt. Everest, finding your dream career, or raising a healthy family, requires a team effort. Jason Steinle's programs bring together the wisdom and experience of our elders with the perspectives and ideas of our peers. Everyone who is questioning what they should do in life must attend his program!"

—Erik Weihenmayer, first blind man to summit Mt. Everest and author of *Touch the Top of the World*

"When I first met Jason I was struck by his passion for life. If you ever have a chance to hear him speak do whatever it takes to be there! You'll be glad you did!"

—Mary LoVerde, author of *Stop Screaming at the Microwave*

"Jason Steinle is a much needed voice on today's college campuses! His programs combine inspiration and practical advice to help shape a better future for today's youth."

—Robert K. Cooper, PhD, author of *The Other 90%*

"Jason Steinle has an extraordinary gift for connecting to his audience. He elegantly informs, entertains, and empowers you to live the life you've always dreamed of. I recommend his programs for anyone ready to take his or her life to the next level!"

—Marilyn Innerfeld, author of *Healing Through Love*

"Jason Steinle's programs are powerful, professional, and content filled. I highly recommend Jason!

—Willie Jolley, voted one of the Outstanding Five Speakers in the World by Toastmasters International and author of *A Setback is a Setup for a Comeback*

QUICK ORDER FORM

Item	Description	Quantity	Unit	Total
#001	UPLOAD EXPERIENCE: Quarterlife Solutions		$19.95/ea.	
	Tax (CO residents add 2.9% sales taxes)		$0.58	
	Shipping and Handling within the continental U.S.		$4.95/first $2.95/add.	
	Total			

Method of Payment:

❏ Check Enclosed (payable to Nasoj Publications, LLC)

❏ Visa   ❏ Mastercard   ❏ American Express

Billing Address: (Please print)

To ensure successful processing of your order, please be sure that the billing address you enter matches the billing address of the credit card you're using.

Name on card: _____

Street Address: _____

City: _____ State: _____ Zip: _____

Email: _____ Phone: _____

Card #: _____ Exp.: _____

Shipping Address: (Please provide if different from billing address.)

Name on card: _____

Street Address: _____

City: _____ State: _____ Zip: _____

Email: _____ Phone: _____

Card #: _____ Exp.: _____

The undersigned purchaser certifies that he or she has read and understands all of the terms conditions on this invoice.

_____
Cardholder's Signature   Date

Please fax your completed form to (303) 670-1001 or mail with payment to
Nasoj Publications, LLC
PO Box 2367
Evergreen, CO 80437 USA
1-888-8UPLOAD

For orders to be shipped outside the continental US, or for bulk orders please contact us online for more information.

WEB: www.UploadExperience.com   EMAIL: Orders@UploadExperience.com

PLEASE ALLOW 2-4 WEEKS FOR DELIVERY